Wild Quest Britain

*A Nature Journey of Discovery Through
England, Scotland & Wales
From Lizard Point to Dunnet Head*

Keith Broomfield

Illustrations by Rob Hands

TIPPERMUIR
· BOOKS LIMITED ·

Wild Quest Britain – Keith Broomfield
Copyright © 2023. All rights reserved.
The right of Keith Broomfield to be identified as the author
of the Work has been asserted in accordance with
the Copyright, Designs & Patents Act 1988.

This first edition published and copyright 2023 by
Tippermuir Books Ltd, Perth, Scotland.

mail@tippermuirbooks.co.uk – www.tippermuirbooks.co.uk.

ISBN 978-1-913836-29-0 (paperback).
A CIP catalogue record for this book is available from the British Library.

Project coordination and editorial by Paul S Philippou.

Cover design by Matthew Mackie.
Illustrations by Rob Hands.
Map by Bernard Chandler

Editorial support: Ajay Close, Julia Garcia, Steve Zajda and Jean Hands.

Co-founders and publishers of Tippermuir Books:
Rob Hands, Matthew Mackie and Paul S Philippou.

Text design, layout, and artwork by Bernard Chandler [graffik].
Text set in Dante MT Std 10.5/14pt with Dante MT Std titling.

Printed and bound by Ashford Colour Press.

'Few things add more enjoyment to a country ramble than a knowledge of the many and varied forms belonging to the animal and vegetable kingdoms that present themselves to notice of the observing wayfarer on every side.'

Richard South, *The Butterflies of the British Isles* (1906)

In memory of Maxwell Cay
(2006-2022)

Author royalties from the sale of this book
will be donated to heart research

ABOUT THE AUTHOR

Keith Broomfield is a well-known Scottish nature writer who has had a passion for wildlife since childhood. A graduate in zoology from the University of Aberdeen, Keith's writing covers virtually every element of the natural world, including flora and fungi, invertebrates, mammals, birds and marine life.

He writes a weekly 'Nature Watch' column for *The Courier* and *The Press & Journal* newspapers, as well as his 'On the Wildside' column for the *Alloa Advertiser,* and occasional pieces for *The Scotsman.* Keith is a trustee/ director of the Forth Rivers Trust, a board member of The Forth Naturalist & Historian and a committee member of the Devon Angling Association.

He has written three books published by Tippermuir Books. His first, *If Rivers Could Sing,* was shortlisted by the Saltire Society in the 2021 Scotland's National Book Awards. His second, *A Scottish Wildlife Odyssey,* is a nature travel journey through Scotland, which received much acclaim in literary reviews. *Wild Quest Britain* is his third.

ACKNOWLEDGEMENTS

The relationship between author and publisher is always an important one and this is my third book under the guidance, encouragement and support of Paul Philippou of Tippermuir Books. I am grateful for his advice throughout the writing process and for the original idea of the book. In equal measure, special thanks to Rob Hands for his excellent illustrations and the midnight oil burned to ensure they were completed within the timeframe.

I would also like to thank Matthew Mackie for yet another splendid book cover; all the team at Tippermuir: Bernard Chandler (graphic design and the map), Steve Zajda and Jean Hands (proof-reading) and Julia Garcia (assistant publisher); and Ajay Close (editorial support).

As ever, my wonderful wife Lynda was a bedrock of encouragement and support when writing *Wild Quest Britain*, and a welcome companion on several parts of my wildlife journey.

Keith Broomfield, August 2023

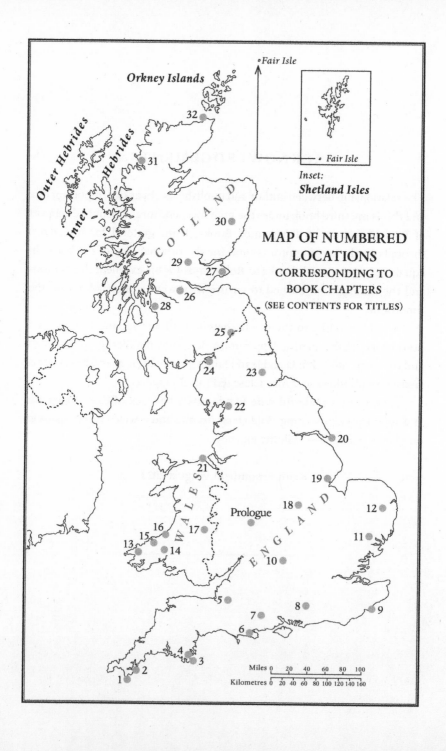

Fair Isle

Orkney Islands

32

31

Outer Hebrides

Inner Hebrides

SCOTLAND

Inset:
Shetland Isles

Fair Isle

30

29

27

26

28

MAP OF NUMBERED
LOCATIONS
CORRESPONDING TO
BOOK CHAPTERS
(SEE CONTENTS FOR TITLES)

25

24

23

22

20

21

19

WALES

18

12

Prologue

17

16

15

13

14

ENGLAND

11

10

5

8

9

7

6

4

3

2

1

Miles 0   20   40   60   80   100

Kilometres 0 20 40 60 80 100 120 140 160

CONTENTS

Prologue

A JOURNEY'S STEPPING-STONE

Early April 2022

It was the chiffchaffs, yes, the singing chiffchaffs that captivated me on that dawn-frosted morning on Hartlebury Common in Worcestershire. Some might maintain that the uncomplicated and repetitive 'chiff-chaff' couplet is monotonous and fails to inspire, but, to many, it has a simple hewn from the rock quality that is one of the beckoning incantations of spring, a sign that nature is on the cusp of remarkable change.

It seemed as if a wave of these small and undistinguished looking warblers had suddenly descended upon Hartlebury Common from their southern European and African wintering grounds, for they abounded all around me. Now, they were venting forth their pent-up emotion for the breeding season ahead, and it was wonderfully addictive – so much so, that I too felt part of their inner elation. 'Chiff-chaff, chiff-chaff' is an uncomplicated call yet with a beguiling appeal – a song that encapsulates the very essence of nature.

Chiffchaffs, Hartlebury Common

Chiffchaff is a poetic and onomatopoeic name, and one that slips easily off the tongue. How their song is described by the written word varies slightly depending upon perception. In the Netherlands, it is known as the 'tjiftjaf', and in Germany, the 'zilpzalp'. It is a call of the wild that transcends borders, and for me that brought additional appeal. This humble greenish little warbler does not recognise arbitrary geographical boundary lines drawn by humanity. For the chiffchaff, the world is one land, one sea and one life-enhancing air to fill the lungs. There is a lesson here for humanity, for boundaries create division and experience tells us that division fosters conflict.

I wandered farther down a wide track and stopped for a while to watch the glowing orange orb of the rising sun as it slowly lifted above the mist-laden eastern horizon. A green woodpecker yodelled from somewhere in the near distance. It is a distinctive and ringing call, traditionally described as a 'yaffle', which is also an alternative name for this striking green, iridescent plumaged bird with a startling scarlet cap. However, an 'Alpine yodel' is a much better reflection of the actuality of the call, and in my mind, it is like the repetitive 'pew, pew, pew' of an osprey.

Green Woodpecker, Hartlebury Common

This osprey reflection brought a momentary longing in my mind for the silver-sparkled lochs and lochans of central Perthshire, where fond memories abound of close encounters with these fish hawks, which wheel in the sky like white-winged spirits of a Highland spring.

The musing on Perthshire was an inadvertent thought thrown upon the consciousness by subliminal angst, for Scotland is my home, and like the migratory chiffchaffs, I too was embarking on an adventure of discovery. After having authored *A Scottish Wildlife Odyssey*, a nature travelogue through Scotland, publisher Tippermuir Books was keen for me to write a similar book focusing on England. It was a compelling idea, but just an initial thought and no more than that. The more we considered it, the more our inclination evolved into the mind of the chiffchaff and to throw asunder borders. Why not make it a wildlife journey through the island of Britain, from Cornwall in the southwest, up through Wales and the rest of England and finishing in the far north of Scotland?

Thus, the seed was sown, and as is often the way of things, journey's start did not begin where originally anticipated, for rather than Cornwall, I was treading carefully along this attractive common in Worcestershire, with its patchwork of trees, gorse and cattle-grazed grass. The reason was prosaic and down to practicality, for travelling from my home in Scotland to Cornwall over 800 km away in one day held little appeal, and as such, Worcestershire became a convenient halfway stopover point for a night's rest.

As it transpired this was the perfect stepping-stone, bringing my thoughts into perspective of the diverse landscape and appeal of Britain. The journey was going to pull me out of my comfort zone, with the opportunity to explore many parts of the land I had never visited before; unfamiliar places, new experiences and new creatures and plants to enthral me. I would be an explorer in my home island – and that held an enticing appeal, which caused a surge of excitement to course through my veins.

The sun rose higher into the sky above Hartlebury Common and the first early-morning dog walkers began to appear. I craved solitude to enjoy the moment, so I veered down a small path, and followed another, and then one more, before biding time below a lone crab apple that materialised before me like a welcoming haven. After a long winter, the awakening colours of spring was a sheer joy, and no more so than the emerging and delicate, blousy white flowers of this small tree. The intricate folds and tucks of the petals had been carefully crafted by the hand of nature, with each flowerhead creating a rippled, creamy sea of entrancement. I hoped the late-season frost would not diminish the vigour of the flowers in the days to come, as sometimes happens with cultivated apple trees. I suspected not, for crab apples are wild and native and have evolved over the millennia to cope with rapid fluctuations in spring weather.

In some ways, Hartlebury Common embodied the soul of Britain. For over 5,000 years, it has been shaped by human activities from nomadic hunter gatherers, through many centuries of common grazing, to the extraction of sand in the eighteenth and nineteenth centuries. During the Second World War, it was used as a defensive and military training site. The signs of humanity are all around that began from the earliest of times, and which rapidly gathered pace over the centuries, resulting in the landscape of today.

Crab Apple Blossom,
Hartlebury Common

I soon reached the top of an escarpment that looked down upon Stourport-on-Severn and farther beyond towards the blue-misted Malvern Hills. The sweet cascading song of a willow warbler drifted across the frost-pinched air. It was a beautiful and bewitching song, contrasting sharply with the simpleness of its close cousin, the chiffchaff. *How could two such similar-looking warblers have evolved completely different songs?* They exhibit contrasting behaviour too, with the chiffchaff arriving upon our shores a couple of weeks before the willow warbler.

Another question arose in my mind. *Do these earlier-arriving chiffchaffs have a competitive advantage over willow warblers because they can establish territories at an earlier stage in the breeding season?* I do not know if that is the case, but that is part of the strong allure of nature, always throwing up perennial conundrums. With Cornwall now beckoning, I knew instinctively this was going to be a journey of continual questions and few answers – and that held an irresistible attraction which was gloriously tantalising.

Chapter 1

A COAST OF LIFE & DEATH

Early April 2022, Cornwall

On flickering wings, a swallow swept in from over the white-flecked sea, bobbing and spiralling like a fragile scrap of wind-blown confetti. It tumbled over the steep clifftop between Kynance Cove and Lizard Point and then glided low over the rabbit-grazed grass and wheeled back round again in a wide arc.

Swallows, The Lizard Peninsula

This swallow was a windblown miracle and I sensed the inner joy it must have felt having started its journey several weeks before in southern Africa and having now made landfall in Cornwall. I inwardly pieced together the swallow's possible route, which may have begun in among herds of fly-buzzed zebras and elephants in the Okavango Delta in northern Botswana. Then, it may have crossed the impenetrable rainforests of the Congo towards the drier regions of the Sahel before the ultimate challenge of a hazardous crossing over the sun-baked and forbidding Sahara Desert.

The final leg across Europe would have proved less daunting, but nonetheless hold considerable hazard, especially if a cold snap were to have taken grip, which would delay the final advancement. There would have been several options for their home run – perhaps crossing the Mediterranean Sea near the Strait of Gibraltar and up through Spain and France, before making the final short hop across the English Channel to reach Lizard Point; the southernmost point of the island of Britain. Equally possible, it may have crossed the Mediterranean from Tunisia and onto Sicily before flying up mainland Italy and over the snowy Alps and onto Cornwall. It was such a small and vulnerable bird, but one that had seen and experienced so much, each day of life representing unimaginable challenge and danger.

It was the early days of April and my first swallow of the year. I revelled in its slender, blue-glossed form as it circled the clifftop several more times, as if in a celebratory lap of honour as it rode the air currents with consummate ease. *Did it have much farther to go, or was the intention to nest here in the southwest of England?* Swallows are renowned as being real homebirds, loyal to the area where they were born, but nothing in nature is ever set in stone, and despite the genetic imprinting that drives the urge to return to their place of birth, there must be the temptation when passing through Spain, France or Italy to nest there, just as so many other swallows do. This would keep the long migration journey slightly shorter and enable earlier nesting. The mild, wet summers of Britain, however, hold their own special appeal: the landscape is rich in flying insects and, for a brief few months, a very productive place for a swallow to raise a family or two. Much better to resist the European Continent's superficial honeypot attractions and instead head to the land of one's creation, where local knowledge can also prove important over each passing year of a swallow's short life.

Suddenly, a small, greyish bird bounded in a short, fluttering flight ahead of me, its white-flashed rump catching the sun, and quickly alighted on top of a grey, lichen-encrusted boulder. It was a male wheatear, with his distinctive black face-masked head. Another early migrant, newly arrived from tropical Africa via France, he flicked his prominent white and black tail nervously for a second or two, before taking to the air once more to swoop down a grassy gully. I peered over the edge of the gully in hope of catching sight of him once more, but he had slipped away among a field of tumbled boulders, his greyish plumage merging seamlessly within the starkness of the landscape.

The sea air was invigorating, a light and airy breeze that tingled the senses, and which was aided and abetted by a lukewarm sun that shone down upon reflective waves. It was impossible not to feel buoyed by the drama of this dramatic Cornish peninsula which juts out into the English Channel. The jagged coast was blessed with a wonderful array of names for every headland, cove, creek, skerry and rock, a storybook of history and language, and no doubt of tragedy. I glanced at my map and randomly reeled a selection of names off in my mind – Rill Ledges, Asparagus Island, Mulvin and Polpeor Cove. Farther north up the coast towards the fishing hamlet of Mullion Cove lay Pigeon Ogo, Pedn Crifton, Velvet Rock and Predannack Head. This was a wild place where over the millennia, nature and humanity coexisted in mutual but fearful respect. One could almost feel the eerie presence of the tragic souls lost at sea in fishing accidents and shipwrecks, and the whole aura of the environment was emotionally moving in a strange, spiritual way.

The signs of spring were not just confined to the newly-arrived swallows and wheatears, for my eyes were continually drawn to the wildflowers that adorned the clifftops, especially the drifts of the creamy bell-like flowers of sea campion, a sprawling, low-set plant perfectly adapted to cope with the worst of coastal storms that can suddenly whip through the air during any month of the year.

I bent down to examine their exquisite flowerheads in more detail; to appreciate their intricate construction of flat white petals held upon a bulbous, balloon-like sac, which are in fact the sepals fused together, the part of the plant which typically protects the bud or supports the flower.

The closely-related bladder campion is so-called because the sac, or calyx as it is known, can be likened to a bladder. Sea campion is an extraordinary-looking plant when seen up close. The calyx is gently adorned with mauve veins, which have the appearance of deftly-applied scribblings. Sea campion is also known as 'dead man's bells', 'witches thimbles' and 'Devil's hatties', so despite its beauty, this is a plant associated with evil, and according to folklore, the plant would bring death if picked. I wondered whether sea campion and the dangerous seas nearby had become intrinsically associated over the centuries into the mindset of the inhabitants as they toiled the land and fished the seas, or engaged in other more nefarious activities such as smuggling.

Many other wildflowers abounded, including scurvygrass with its miniscule white petals, and pink nodding patches of thrift, or sea pink as it is sometimes known. The leaves of scurvygrass are rich in vitamin C and the plant is so-termed because in the past it was widely used by sailors to prevent the onset of scurvy. In seventeenth-century England, it was fashionable to partake in a tonic made from scurvygrass every morning, much in the same way as we would enjoy a glass of fruit juice today.

Sea Campion

The compact pink flower-cushions of thrift which dotted the ground nearby looked so delicate, but this plant is a true stalwart being able to thrive in harsh maritime environments of scouring sea winds and gaining tenure in the shallowest of soils. Their tightly-packed leaves help the plant conserve water in the salty air.

As I neared Lizard Point, offshore reefs and skerries broke the sea's surface, where swirling currents and powerful tidal flows whipped the water into a white-frothed spume. These reefs would be incredibly rich in marine life, and my mind delved under the water conjuring an imaginary vision of vibrant and colourful sea squirts and sponges clinging to steep rock faces, while shoals of bass and pollack flashed by on the hunt for small fish and unwary invertebrates such as crabs and worms. The undersea world is a passion of mine and I hankered to snorkel in these rich Cornish waters, but the time for that would come shortly, and for the moment it was the coastal scenery that absorbed my attention.

On reaching Lizard Point, I ventured farther on towards the eastern flank of the adjacent Housel Bay. Jackdaws wheeled in the updrafts and skylarks sang and soared on quivering wings into the wide blue heavens. I carefully examined the jackdaws through my binoculars in case of mistaken identity and the possibility that some of them might be rare choughs. Despite my persistent searching, no choughs materialised, but such was the magic of watching the jackdaws cavort in the air as they eagerly investigated their nesting crevices in the cliffs, seeking out the rare from the common, it did not matter. Nature was busily bustling below me, and I could not have felt more at ease with the world.

I sat on a wooden bench by the coastal path, where I reflected briefly upon the chough. These scarce crow-like birds with their long, red-curved beaks recolonised Lizard Point in 2001, after being absent for almost three decades. Now there are over twenty pairs and there is real hope that numbers will continue to grow. They are fussy in their habits and like to forage together in small groups for worms and other invertebrates on the short grassland near the coast, and to nest on the nearby cliffs. Their future in Cornwall, and elsewhere, depends to a substantial extent on the cooperation between conservationists and landowners to ensure their specific habitat requirements are met.

Such was the lure of the Cornish cliffs, I returned repeatedly for several days. One visit included Land's End, for no other reason that it is the most southwesterly point of mainland Britain, which held its own special appeal. Out at sea, gannets plunged into the water, their wings swept back just before impact, to create a streamlined torpedo shape that could propel downwards at great speed and considerable force. The wind was gusty and white horses rolled across the wave crests, before folding and dissipating into the grey-churned water. It is difficult to imagine how a gannet could even spot a fish in such tempestuous conditions, and then have the skill and agility to dive into the sea from a good height and pluck its prey from the water. In the eye of the gannet, the world must appear vastly different from ours, so much more detailed and varied.

On another day, a clifftop walk took me to Mullion Cove on the west side of the Lizard, where piercing hailstones clattered down from darkened clouds, which made my mind ponder further upon the swallow I had glimpsed only so recently. Arriving in southern England in early April is a risky business for swallows, wheatears, warblers and the like, for the unforgiving hand of winter is often reluctant to relinquish its grip. A prolonged cold snap can easily prove fatal for early spring migrants, given that insects will hunker down and become difficult to catch.

A coastal walk backdropped by turquoise seas from Kennack Sands to the village of Coverack on the eastern side of the Lizard was rewarded by some of the largest drifts of dog violets I have ever encountered, spreading along the clifftops in a dreamy purple haze. Many of the clumps prospered where fires had recently borne the ground clear, and it was apparent that the violets benefited from the removal of the thick and heavy cover of gorse. Violet is a transfixing word, which describes the flower so perfectly, but the prefix 'dog' is unnecessarily demeaning. In the past, 'dog' was a derogatory term used in nature nomenclature, for example dogwood, because its berries are unpalatable. For dog violet, it is a reference to the flowers being scentless, which is indeed the case, but the blooms shine in so many other ways and they are one of our most attractive early spring plants.

The violet is an enduring wildflower, able to withstand windswept clifftops, and cold and frosty early spring days. The nineteenth-century English poet, John Clare, in his poem, 'Holywell', noted:

> And just to say that spring was come,
> The violet left its woodland home,
> And, hermit-like, from storms and wind
> Sought the best shelter it could find,
> 'Neath long grass banks, with feeble flowers
> Peeping faintly purple flowers:

The north coast of Cornwall brought its own irresistible pull, including a short visit to the busy seaside town of St Ives. The sun was shining, and with the Easter holiday season about to get underway, throngs of people were already bustling the seafront. Incredibly, in among the feet of these holidaymakers on the street pavements were small groups of turnstones, ducking this way and that on pattering feet as they foraged for inadvertently-dropped fast-food scraps.

Turnstones are small and enchanting wading birds, which breed in Arctic Greenland and Canada, and in only a few weeks' time, these birds at St Ives would set off for the tundra. It was difficult to imagine a starker contrast in habitat, true wild birds of the high Arctic yet at ease in the presence of tourists in this bustling Cornish resort. Intriguingly, the holidaymakers paid scant regard to the turnstones dashing fleet-of-foot about them and they were being regarded in much the same familiar way as house sparrows or feral pigeons.

The adage 'if you don't look, you won't see' is one of the hallmarks of our awareness of nature. Look and you will always see, for nature's hold is everywhere, even in our most urbanised areas.

Later that day, I ventured a short distance farther up the northwestern corner of Cornwall to the wonderfully wild coastline at Godrevy, near the town of Hayle, where rollers crashed along the vast expanse of sandy beach that stretched towards the towering headland of Godrevy Point. Just beyond the point, grey seals lay hauled out on the pebbly shore of Mutton Cove, resting after a spell of fishing. The land is owned by the National Trust and there is a viewing platform on the clifftop from where it is possible to observe seals without disturbing them. Along the tourist-magnet Cornish coast, coves such as this, protected from human activity, are attractive for seals looking for safe places to pup and rest. These seals looked contented with their lot, rolling languidly on their sides, their bodies fat and plump from enjoying the sea's rich bounty.

The names of some of the nearby inlets and other coastal features once again drew my attention – Hell's Mouth and Deadman's Cove shone out – and as a wind-tumbled raven swept past me, an involuntary shiver coursed down my spine. This was a place full of wondrous life, but in the past, like much of the Cornish coast, it was inextricably associated with death.

Chapter 2

EXPLORING THE WONDERS OF
MAWGAN CREEK

Early April 2022, Cornwall

While the drama of the coastal cliffs absorbed much of my time in Cornwall, I became equally enchanted by Mawgan Creek, a small muddy offshoot of the Helford River. The cottage I resided in for my week-long stay in Cornwall overlooked the creek, which provided a wonderful vantage point to observe the comings and goings of the creatures that prospered within its shallow hold. Each morning and evening, the relentless power of the tide flowed over the mudbanks to fill this side-channel of the Helford River, and then a few hours later, streamed back out again. The tide orchestrated the creek, and the water birds that lived there were in intimate harmony with every nuance and quirk of the tidal flow and had adapted their behaviour to suit the daily pattern of the river.

At night, under starry skies, the creek intoned a wondrous resonance as mallards gently quacked from watery margins and the gentle breeze rustled bare treetops, where old storm-damaged branches creaked and groaned as if in mutual sympathy with one another. Moorhens whinnied and tawny owls 'hooed, hooed' like quivering flutes. When dawn broke, the lifting of the shroud of darkness revealed herons stalking the banksides and herring gulls squabbling amongst themselves in the water.

The Helford River flows into the English Channel several kilometres south of Falmouth and is one of several estuaries in Cornwall that indent deep into the surrounding countryside like creeping tendrils, feeling their way into every tuck and fold of the rolling landscape. The rivers Fowey and Fal are notable estuaries on the south coast, while those that stand out on the north are the River Hayle, near St Ives, and the River Camel, which enters the sea at Padstow. As is the case with more exposed parts of the rugged Cornish coast, the names of the side creeks found within these estuaries roll deliciously off the tongue – Restronguet Creek, Ruan Creek and Tressillian Creek, to name but a few.

From first sight, I was instantly smitten by Mawgan Creek, and like a developing affair of the heart, this initial fancy quickly grew into something deeper. This was a special place in my eyes, bounded by thick broadleaved woodland, where gnarled oaks and other trees tapped their roots right down to the water's edge, drawn by the low salinity of the brackish water. The creek was an interface between intertidal and terrestrial fauna and flora, the two environments merging as one – different in nature, but with an overriding compatibility. In some places, tumbled trees laid on the tidal mud and at high water their twisted branches acted like reefs, where invertebrates and fish sought shelter, and which provided places for cormorants to rest and hold their open wings like dark sentinel crucifixes. Farther in the distance, on the far side of the Helford River, a thick swathe of woodland swept up a hillside where the treetops had been sculpted into a rounded dome by the prevailing wind.

Redshanks & A Greenshank

As the week progressed, the behaviour of a small group of redshanks which inhabited the creek increasingly intrigued me. When the tide was out, there was never any hint of these small, greyish and red-legged wading birds, with the exposed and glutinous mudbanks being empty and largely bereft of obvious life. Presumably, at this stage in the tidal cycle, the redshanks had ventured nearer the open coast where the pickings were richer. All this changed as the tide flooded back in, when the sinuous and narrow water channel that carved its way through the middle of the mudflats began to noticeably rise. The banks of the channel (which was the outflow of the stream that emptied into the creek) were steep and it took an hour or so for the incoming tide to breach the upper margin, after which the water quickly washed over to inundate the rest of the shallow basin in a matter of minutes.

Redshank

This rising water that determinedly filled the winding channel acted like a cue, for it hastened the arrival of the redshanks, flying in on grey-flashed wings and alighting on the mud banks in a state of perceptible excitement. It was always the same small group of six birds, that appeared day after day, and which were invariably accompanied by a lone greenshank. The greenshank is similar in appearance to a redshank, but slightly larger and with lighter-grey plumage, and as the name suggests, has greenish legs.

Greenshank

Greenshanks are much scarcer than redshanks and given the absence of others of its own kind on this part of the Helford River, this individual had sought out the company of an avian cousin. The science tells us that this makes sense, for there is safety in numbers, and a group of birds has more eyes to watch-out for a predator than a lone individual. I suspect there are other reasons at work too, and it was entirely plausible this greenshank found mental comfort in having companions. Communication between the two species would be possible too, for while the greenshank and redshank have different vocalisations, the greenshank would quickly learn the meaning of redshank alarm and other purposeful calls. It is a principle found throughout nature – if a blackbird in woodland utters its alarm call, other songbirds in the vicinity instantly become on heightened alert.

As the tide flooded-in, worms and other invertebrates stirred into activity and rose to the surface of the ooze from their subterranean muddy lairs. This was the opportunity the redshanks and their lone greenshank compatriot were waiting for, and they quickly moved into action, patrolling the spreading edge of the waterline and quickly snapping up small creatures as they emerged from the mud or began to filter feed. For a brief few minutes, just after the tide had spilled over the channel to cover the mudflats in their entirety, the birds waded thigh deep, giving the impression they were swimming. Soon, the depth became too much, and like a flight of teal leaping from the water, they took to the air and alighted by the edge of the creek to rest for a while.

Mawgan Creek held other natural treasures, including shelduck that methodically sifted the mud for tiny invertebrates by sweeping their bills rapidly from side-to-side in the same manner as a flamingo feeding in a shallow lagoon. A little egret was another regular visitor that stalked the rising water of the channel for small flounders, eels and grey mullet. It was an elegant bird with its snowy-white plumage and long-streamer crest, but always wary, taking flight whenever I approached too closely. On initial consideration, it might seem strange that egrets should evolve startling white plumage, which makes them stand out conspicuously. Yet, for hunting, it is the perfect camouflage, for a fish peering up through the surface of the water would find it difficult to discern the white body of an egret against a pale sky.

Little Egret

The expansion in range of the little egret into the British Isles is remarkable and is part of a northwards trend exhibited by many birds and insects in recent decades. As an enthusiastic teenage birdwatcher in the 1970s, the little egret was a bird I associated with the marshes and lagoons of the Camargue in the French Mediterranean, or in the Algarve in Portugal, rather than a Cornish mud-bank. This most delicate and attractive little heron has undergone a quite phenomenal northwards movement over the past 40 years that has seen it become an established breeder in England and Wales and a regular visitor to Scotland. The reasons behind this change in distribution are uncertain but most likely has been facilitated by climate change.

The weather during my week in Cornwall was unsettled, with the sun sometimes shining bright, and at other times a heavy darkling sky hung over the creek like a brooding blanket, where squalls whipped the water and ruffled the surface in a concertina of ripples that sent waves lapping onto the shore.

I was keen to find out more about the invertebrates that inhabited the creek, so one evening, just before the incoming tide, I set a lightweight collapsible creel that I often carry when on nature expeditions and baited it with tinned mackerel. On hauling the creel the following morning, it bulged with green shore crabs, about 30 animals in all. They were feisty creatures when held in the hand and sported an attractive shell patterning. Rather than being green as the name suggests, several of the crabs in the creel were adorned with splashes of turquoise on the back of the shell and red-orange on the legs and claws. It took time to carefully extract each crab from the trap. The tactic for avoiding a sore nip is to hold the crab between forefinger and thumb from the back of its carapace, which renders the claws powerless to reach a finger or fold of skin. With so many crabs in the creel, however, it was impossible to extract them all without experiencing at least a few painful pinches in the process.

Green shore crabs are prolific and represent one of our most important and successful inshore marine creatures. They have cosmopolitan tastes and will feed upon pretty much anything they can get their claws on, including molluscs, worms and small crustaceans, as well as being avid scavengers. In turn, they are preyed upon by gulls, eider ducks, otters and fish such as cod. Herring and sandeels will feast upon them in their larval planktonic stage, and as such, shore crabs are a fundamental ecological keystone of our inshore waters. Although marine living in the main, shore crabs also thrive in brackish, low-salinity waters, such as found at Mawgan Creek, which further underlines their innate versatility in exploiting a range of inshore and tidal habitats. They are crustacean pioneers, reaching any part of the country that has at least a hint of brine.

On a wider scale, such success has its downsides, and in Australia, for example, green shore crabs are an invasive and unwelcome foreign interloper from Europe, having first arrived in the ballast of wooden ships in the late 1800s, and are now threatening native species there, as well as impacting upon oyster farms.

Mawgan Creek and its environs held many other attractions. Each dawn, and then again shortly before dusk, I wandered along small paths that weaved their way through the woodland that enveloped the creek. Oak, beech, elm, ash and hornbeam were among the mainstay trees, but there were also clusters of Scots pines, and hazel was abundant as a thick under-storey. The woodland was a hypnotically tranquil place where the mind drifted in quiet contemplation as I sought out early spring flowers such as dog violets, primroses and ramsons.

Ivy covered many of the trees, the shiny green leaves sprouting luxuriantly from the thick woody tendrils that climbed up trunks like coiled steel hawsers. Ivy is an unsung hero of our woodlands, the evergreen, lobed leaves providing shelter for a host of creatures, including invertebrates and nesting and roosting birds. In autumn, ivy's greenish-yellow flowers are avidly sought by pollinating insects, and the small black berries are devoured by birds. It is an evergreen liana that flourishes in deep shade, making it perfectly adapted for life in thick woodland. Ivy is steeped in folklore, with early herbalists believing its berries could vanquish the toxicity of alcohol because of its ability to smother grape vines, and the plant's supposed magical powers were said to be able to ward-off house goblins at Christmas time.

I parted one particularly lush growth of ivy on a tree trunk and plunged my head in deep to become immersed within the dark confines of an ivy's world, where the damp smell of moss and lichens quickly filled my lungs. In this twilight environment, a small beetle scuttled up the bark, safe from the prying eyes of predators and a tiny red mite shone out like a blown-away spark from a fire. It was a secret place, protected from wind and sun, and a little powerhouse of life, which benefited the surrounding woodland to an unimaginable degree.

The woodland very quickly became my daily comfort blanket, and I relished its wildness, providing an opportunity to reflect about nature and our place within it.

One morning as I padded down a narrow path in the wood, a pair of raucous jays screeched loudly before quickly falling silent. Their calls reminded me of autumn when jays are especially noisy. For much of the year these beautiful birds keep themselves to themselves, but in autumn family parties go foraging for acorns and beech nuts – and, oh, what a noisy business it is!

For such a stunning bird, the jay has the most awful call. It is not even worth contemplating some redeeming quality in the sharp strident hissing screech that conjures an image of an incredibly bad-tempered creature that likes nothing better than to spend its time bickering and scolding. Rather than being in a perpetual state of strangled torment, it is simply a case of nature not endowing jays with a more musical repertoire. In jay-speak these raucous calls are in all likelihood an indication of happy birds collecting autumn's rich harvest from the forest floor.

Jays are great hoarders and will bury nuts and seeds over considerable distances. It is thought that the jay takes careful note of obvious landmarks such as bushes and boulders near where each acorn is stored so that they can be found later in winter when food is less abundant. The sheer number of seeds involved means that a reasonable proportion will never be retrieved, and the bird plays an important role in the spread of oak and other trees to new areas, much in the same way as squirrels do.

One day, I ventured a short distance down the coast to where the Helford River flows out into the sea to the attractive village of Porthallow, with its shingle beach bounded on either side by low cliffs. The rock shelves that bordered the northern edge of the beach looked ideal for snorkelling, especially since the weather on the previous two days had been calm, resulting in settled, crystal clear water.

Donned in wetsuit, mask and flippers, I slipped into the water and let out an involuntarily yelp of pleasure, for this was my first snorkel of the year and becoming immersed once more in the magic of the underwater world made my heart sing with joy. There was plenty of marine life about, including corkwing wrasse and a fast-swimming garfish that shot along just below the surface of the water like a mini torpedo. Garfish are curious-looking fish – elongated and with long beak-like jaws. They are open-water creatures that generally swim close to the surface as they seek out plankton and small fish such as young herring and sandeels to feed upon. Sometimes they hunt in shoals, but whenever I have come upon them in the past, it has always been as individuals or in pairs. They have the habit of jumping out of the water when pursuing their prey or when they themselves are being hunted by larger fish.

A large ballan wrasse glided below, and on glimpsing me, it carefully sidled up to a large rock on the seabed and pressed its body against it in the hope of making itself inconspicuous. Wrasses are an endearing group of fish. They are weak swimmers, preferring to use their cryptic colouration and slow movements to prevent detection. The ichthyologist, James Travis-Jenkins, in *The Fishes of the British Isles* (1925), noted that their flesh is 'little esteemed' and as such they are a fish of no commercial interest, although they are often caught by sea anglers.

When younger, I typically dived deep when snorkelling, but nowadays I am less gung-ho and more aware of my body limitations, mainly keeping dives to only a few metres depth, although occasionally I will still throw caution to the wind. Generally, I prefer to potter in the shallows where there is frequently so much more to see than deeper down. This ploy worked well at Porthallow, and in one rock fissure a startling strawberry anemone beamed out at me – a large crimson blob with pale yellow-green speckles, which resembled the tiny pips on the skin of a strawberry.

Sea anemones belong to a large group of animals known as cnidarians that typically feature a body with a single opening surrounded by tentacles, which contain stinging cells that are used to both immobilise prey and for defence. When rock pooling, I can never resist the temptation to draw my finger over the tentacles of closely-related beadlet anemones, which are more common than strawberry anemones. The tentacles are sticky to the touch, a sensation partially caused by the anemone firing stinging cells in response to the probing intrusion of a finger, although the stingers are not strong enough to penetrate the skin and be felt.

I pushed my body away from the large rock where the strawberry anemone nestled and slowly swam over a deeper expanse of water. On the seabed, a large, pinkish crab slowly crawled through the wavy tangles of seaweed. It was a spider crab, its gangly long legs carefully picking a route through the maze of rocks and seaweed. I followed it for a while, engrossed by its jerky movements and giving occasional kicks of my flippers to keep on station above it. My lack of vigorous swimming and body movement soon brought a shiver of coldness running down my body, and I reluctantly decided to call it a day and drifted back to shore.

On hauling myself out of the water onto the shingle beach, I pulled off my mask and wetsuit hood and gazed back out across the calm water. A swirl momentarily broke the surface, leaving behind a circular spread of ripples, which quickly diminished. I couldn't be sure, but it looked like a garfish was on the hunt and had just made a predatory pass at a shoal of tiny fish.

Chapter 3

THE TALE OF A LOST VILLAGE & A BUNTING THAT HAS RETURNED FROM THE BRINK

Early April 2022, Devon

The entrance of spring reveals a new dawn,
Soft morning rays glance the blue liquid lawn,
A kiss of warmth on the face of the land,
An injection of life following winter's frost hand.
The chatter of young voices fills the air,
A summer's nursery, born without care,
Blossoming colours, radiant in their splendour,
Complete this mosaic of nature's wonder.

'Awakening' by Steve Edmonds

On open, sharp-edged wings, the female peregrine soared above me and hung motionless in the air, constantly trimming her flight feathers to maintain pinpoint position by using eddies from the sea breeze that spiralled-up from the clifftop.

The falcon had a ragged tail, possibly because she had been incubating eggs and the feathers had become frayed within the restricted confines of her eyrie. My first inclination was the falcon was hunting for prey, such as rock doves or jackdaws, but when brought under focus with my binoculars it was apparent that she was instead observing my every move through piercing eyes. Perhaps she was curious by my presence, but the clifftops here at Start Point in Devon are frequented by many walkers and the falcon would be used to the presence of people. Or maybe she was interested as to whether my movements might inadvertently flush songbirds from the surrounding gorse, giving an opportunity to swoop down and strike.

My eyeballing of the peregrine seemed to unnerve her, and realising she was now the subject of my own scrutiny, closed her wings and under the inexorable power of gravity swept away in a long shallow dive. I waited in case she might swoop back up in the air again, but she had spirited herself away, and the sky remained blue and empty.

I walked on. While Cornwall is wild and rugged, Devon is more benign in nature, the environment that little bit softer, more rounded and without the hard edges. Backing onto the coast are rolling, verdant pastures, intersected by hedgerows and numerous copses. It is an undulating landscape of green, grassy domes and spurs, all interlinked in harmonious unison to create a greater whole. Devon has a welcoming embrace that draws one in like a bee to a honeypot, an irresistible pull that becomes empowering and totally addictive.

I was staying at the charming hamlet of Hallsands, which lies close to Start Point on the south coast. It was a delightful spot, where the white-frothed surge crashed against the shingle beach and the sun-shimmered sea danced in a magical dusting of star-sparkled light. Especially compelling was the coastal walk from Start Point that scrambled westwards to Prawle Point, which unfolded such a treasure trove of natural delights that it was hard to pull myself away and explore other parts of Devon as was my original intention. Here, unusual creatures such as great green bush crickets, digger wasps and the silver-studded blue butterfly thrive; colourful wildflowers include pink-bloomed thrift, yellow kidney vetch and white sea carrot.

Inevitably, I succumbed to the persuasive allure of this corner of Devon and abandoned any thought of significant travel from my home base for the week at Hallsands. *This was as good as it gets*, I mused – much better to enjoy the moment and the location. It was a prescient dawning on the consciousness because the day before in a moment of anguish I had felt an underlying urgency to visit a variety of places in Devon to see as many animal and plant species as time would allow. No, I minded, *My journey should not be a ticking exercise to see the rare and unusual, but more a random dip into Britain's natural wealth to provide a true reflection of the flavour of the land.*

Just south of Hallsands, lies the ruins of the original fishing village of the same name, which collapsed into the sea on a stormy night in January 1917. The entire village was destroyed along with the livelihoods of its inhabitants, reverberations from which are still felt to this day. It is a tragic tale of deception and greed, where the hand of man was responsible for the village's destruction. In the 1890s, the Admiralty wanted to expand the naval dockyard at Keyham, near Plymouth, which resulted in the vast underwater shingle beds in the sea off Hallsands being dredged to provide aggregate for the construction work. The removal of the protective shingle greatly changed the dynamics of the sea currents offshore, which led to unprecedented coastal erosion and the final dramatic end to the village as it tumbled into the sea. The villagers warned of the ticking timebomb that was going to befall them, but were ignored by the dredging company and government, their voices lost in the sea-wind of making money and deflecting blame.

Recounting that fateful night, where miraculously no one died, Edith Patey, a 17-year-old villager, said:

> All of a sudden the walls came toppling down, the floor caved in. We felt like being right in the sea, the roaring waves bouncing over us, the rafters all breaking in. We could see the white waves foaming under the floors.

Human existence and nature go hand-in-hand, and on viewing the remains of the village through my binoculars, I wondered what types of fish had sustained the Hallsands community. I found the answer in Ruth and Frank Milton's book *Sisters Against the Sea* (2005). The fishing was divided between potting for crab and lobster, which went on for most of the year; seine netting, which was seasonal, for bass, grey mullet and mackerel; tuck netting, also described as drag netting, for flatfish such as plaice, dabs and turbot; and trammel netting for bait fish like dogfish and wrasse. Longlines were deployed to hook conger, pollack and rays. Salmon were also caught on their way to the nearby River Dart, although this was strictly controlled by licence and required a special net. Up until the end of the nineteenth century, pilchard and herring were plentiful in the bay.

Today, the shingle beach at Hallsands is a popular base for sea anglers to set off in their specially adapted kayaks to fish with rod and line in the deeper waters offshore. Keen to find out their quarry, and if there had been any change over time, I struck up a conversation with an angler one morning, who told me that the area was renowned for plaice. Other fish frequently caught were turbot, bass and whiting, along with mackerel in season. Later that day, I dived in by the edge of the beach with snorkel and mask and quickly spotted several ballan and corkwing wrasse flickering over the seabed and a glistening shoal of iridescent sand smelts. On rocks close to the shore, black-ringed limpets gained tenure. They are not as frequent as the common limpet, being smaller in size and found mainly in the southwest and Wales.

Backing onto the beach was a large area of reeds fed by a small stream, which emerged as a trickle out onto the shingle where it drained through the pebbles as the beach shelved steeply down to the sea. Beyond the reeds lay three old carp ponds, which were a joy to wander around at dawn and dusk while pipistrelle bats fluttered low over the water and tawnies hooted from nearby trees.

One morning, when exploring a path on the north side of the reeds, a small, dumpy bird spiralled up into a hawthorn, and uttered a short, rapid-fire metallic song. It was a cirl bunting, a nationally rare bird and a relative of the commoner and more widespread yellowhammer. The light was poor, and despite the cirl bunting darkly silhouetted against a grey sky, I managed to discern its distinctive black chin, throat and eye stripe.

Cirl Bunting

Cirl buntings are at the northern edge of their European range in Devon and have specific habitat and climate requirements, which make them vulnerable. Once known as 'village buntings' due to their former abundance, they declined markedly in England and Wales in the twentieth century and by the end of the 1980s there were only around 100 pairs, principally confined to south Devon. It is thought the main drivers for the decline were changes in farming practices, particularly the switch to autumn sowing of cereals and the widespread use of herbicides.

Cirl buntings are remarkably sedentary birds that lack any wanderlust whatsoever, which in turn means their year-round feeding and nesting requirements need to lie close together over a small area. They thrive best on diverse mixed-farming systems that deliver a patchwork of different habitats, including invertebrate-rich grasslands and winter stubbles rich in seeds. The decline of traditional mixed-farming practices in modern times led to the loss of such key foraging areas.

From around the turn of the millennium, carefully targeted habitat improvements funded by agri-environment schemes and implemented by conservation-minded farmers has seen numbers rise and there are now over 1,000 pairs in south Devon. The recovery is an inspiring tale, which reminded me of a similar initiative in the Hebrides to boost the flagging corncrake population. There are huge financial pressures to maximise agricultural efficiency, yet often at great cost to the environment. *How do you balance the importance of food production and food security, against the need for a healthy environment that keeps our air clean and water pure, and which delivers the very oxygen of life?* The example of the cirl bunting shows such balance can be achieved with proper planning, and of course money, to ensure farming livelihoods are not diminished whilst ensuring nature can thrive.

With such thoughts coursing through my mind, the cirl bunting fluttered away and disappeared into a stand of willow carr that fringed the reedbed. Carefully skirting around a group of inquisitive cows in an open pasture, I was able to complete a circular route back to Hallsands, taking a small high-banked country lane on my return leg. These lanes proliferate throughout Devon and Cornwall, comprising a sprawling and interlinking network of hedge banks that glow and shimmer in springtime from a profusion of wildflowers. In summer, they are thick with nettles and bramble tangles, and in winter hold a rich bounty of seeds and haws that are feasted upon by finches, bank voles and wood mice.

I stopped to examine a section of the lane bank in more detail. The flora was diverse – herb-Robert, primrose, dog violet, hart's-tongue fern, bluebells and alexanders all registered in my mind on the first initial glance, and there were the green shoots of emerging nettles. The bank was topped with hawthorn, blackthorn and elder, which would burst with nutritious berries in late summer and autumn. These lane banksides are an eclectic equivalent of glade, meadow, and open-scrub, all wrapped into one and which stretch for an unimaginable number of kilometres throughout the southwest of England like an intricate, sprawling network of life-enhancing capillaries.

These lane margins are among the single most important habitats in this part of England, proliferating with life and safe from development. England's country lanes are an integral part of the wild beating heart of the country, acting as wildlife corridors that link habitats and provide places for plants to prosper and animals to forage, breed and shelter. As if in confirmation of that fact, a blackcap sang in the trees above me, and a cock greenfinch launched into the air on parachute wings in a short, song flight, his wings fluttering in slow, exaggerated beats like a large butterfly. The poet, Francis Duggan, described the accompanying song as 'the beauty born of nature for us all to enjoy'. The blackcap piped-up once more, a rich fluty song, which was delivered with startling boldness; there was no gentle warm up or soft introductory tones, just an incredible short blast of high intensity music.

One morning, thick mist shrouded the shore at Hallsands, but there was the promise that a lingering sun high in the sky would soon burn it back. With this in mind, I took the coastal path northwards that leads to the nearby village of Beesands. It was a gentle and pleasant route despite the mist reining back the sea views. To the north of Beesands lay the small, shallow lake of Widdicombe Ley, where the mist began to lift enough for me to glimpse a great-crested grebe sitting on its floating nest by a reedy island, with its mate patrolling the water nearby.

After watching the waterfowl on the water for a short while, I ambled back towards the seafront where a male black redstart suddenly materialised before my eyes and perched on one of the coastal block enforcements that are feature of this part of the coast. Small numbers of black redstarts reside around English coasts in winter, although I suspected this one had just newly arrived from France on migration, the mist forcing him down into Beesands. He was remarkably tame and flicked his red tail with real enthusiasm. Black redstarts are about the size of a robin, with the male in his breeding garb exhibiting charcoal-grey plumage.

Although black redstarts are widespread in summer in Europe, especially around settlements in upland areas like the Alps, they are scarce breeders in Britain, with the first recorded nesting in 1923. They have developed a penchant for nesting around buildings, and bomb sites in London provided abundant nesting sites during the Second World War and in the immediate aftermath. Breeding numbers dwindled in the decades thereafter and it is currently a scarce breeding bird in Britain.

This black redstart provided a good illustration of the frequent uncertainties that hallmark nature. Here was a bird widespread in Europe and associated with humans, and where there are many apparently suitable areas for it to thrive in Britain – yet it does not. *Why should that be so?* I do not know the answer, but many creatures and plants depend upon subtle nuances in the environment for their survival, some of which we are unaware of, and the black redstart is just one example of this. This, of course, is a concern because if we do not know the specific requirements and needs of individual species, it is nigh-on impossible to develop conservation plans to ensure their protection should numbers ever begin to diminish.

Chapter 4

ELUSIVE WARBLERS & A DIP INTO THE TREASURES OF SLAPTON LEY

Early April 2022, Devon

A sharp burst of song exploded from the reeds beside me – a slow-starting 'tu-rit, tu-rit', followed by a rapid-fire 'tu-rit, tu-rit, tu-rit'. I scrutinised the reedbed but there was no sign of the bird that had made this impossibly loud call. I wandered farther along the track by the lake at Slapton Ley, and then in a hedge bank tangle another bird burst forth – 'tu-rit, tu-rit', a short pause, and then 'tu-rit, tu-rit, tu-rit'.

Cetti's Warbler

They were Cetti's warblers, elusive birds that skulk in reeds and thick vegetation by the margins of ditches and lakes. These little brown warblers pack an almighty musical punch and every so often let rip with the most stunning short bursts of song. I was determined to catch a glimpse of this musical maestro and stood my ground in the hope the bird might appear. A brown, blurry movement momentarily caught the corner of my eye in among the bramble stems, but it slipped away again into the dark, tangled depths.

Frustrated, I moved on. A short while later, however, the music burst forth once more, although there was still nary a sight of the songster despite my eyes scanning every inch of scrub. I waited, and then there was a barely perceptible movement as the elusive warbler scuttled through the undergrowth and briefly paused in a gap between the foliage. It was a snapshot moment, no more than that, but long enough to appreciate the form of the bird. It was similar in appearance to a small nightingale but without the russet tail, and exhibited warm-brown upperparts and softer, greyish tones beneath. As quick as it had appeared, it was gone, scurrying through the dark world of bramble tangles like a mysterious troglodyte.

The Cetti's warbler has undergone a similar northward range expansion as the little egret in recent decades, first arriving from France in the 1970s. Now, they are ubiquitous in the south of England, their clamouring songs ringing out wherever there is water nearby, whether from damp ditches, tangled scrub or reedbeds. Unlike most other British warblers which are spring and summer visitors, the Cetti's warbler is a year-round resident. I wonder whether their presence impacts upon sedge warblers and reed warblers that live in the same kind of damp margins. For example, the Cetti's warbler will have a head start over establishing the best breeding territories compared to sedge and reed warblers, which don't arrive upon our shores until mid-April. It is an interesting question worth researching, although as far as I am aware, there is no indication that the presence of the Cetti's is detrimental to other warblers.

Slapton Ley boasts the largest natural body of freshwater in the southwest of England, a fragile shingle bar dividing the lake from the sea. Located on the English Channel coast several kilometres south of Dartmouth, it is a haven for waterfowl and other wildlife. Managed by the Field Studies Council in partnership with others, Slapton Ley features a mix of habitats, which alongside the lake includes wet meadows and damp woodland, hazel coppice and a tenuous beach that is continuously on the move. The narrow protective shingle bar is vulnerable to storms and could subside at any time, connecting the ley to the sea and creating a completely new environment. It is nature hanging in the balance and on the cusp of huge change should the bar be breached, as it undoubtedly will be one day.

Despite the proximity of the sea, the water in the ley is completely fresh and is home to a rich variety of life. I was keen to gain an insight into the underwater world of the ley, but suspected snorkelling would be frowned upon. A wooden pontoon in one corner of the lake provided a convenient alternative solution. With a bit of dexterity, it was possible, while wearing a face mask, to lie belly-down on the jetty with my upper body hanging-off the edge and head under the water. It proved an effective technique, with the additional bonus that fish were attracted to the water beneath the pontoon because of the shelter it offered.

On my first head dunk, a glistening mixed shoal of fish swept by, their orange fins catching the sunlight as they tail-flicked over the thick growth of Canadian pondweed below. There was a profusion of fish, all about 100 to 150 mm long, and it was strangely relaxing to be privy to their random movements. Most were perch and roach, although a few rudd were present too, distinguished from the similar-looking roach by their chunkier bodies.

Perch & Roach

So similar are roach and rudd that they sometimes interbreed, with the resultant fertile hybrids showing intermediate characteristics of the two. I am uncertain what such hybridisation means for the integrity of each species, but no doubt the two have been interbreeding since the dawn of time with little ill effect. Perhaps the mixing and matching of genes is a good thing, enhancing robustness and diversity within the two species.

Perch were similarly numerous, their distinctive, boldly-marked vertical-striped, greenish bodies wavering along the bottom. Although predominately freshwater denizens, the perch in the ley are one species that would be able to withstand the partial inundation of the sea should the beach barrier crumble. Perch can thrive in brackish water and watching these fish reminded me of an occasion many moons ago when snorkelling in the low salinity Baltic Sea where I found perch (and pike) sheltering under a pontoon similar to the one at Slapton Ley. Sticklebacks show similar brackish water toleration.

Each type of fish in the ley adopts their own special niche – roach and rudd, for example, are omnivorous and will eat invertebrates, plants, seeds and other natural detritus. Perch, on the other hand, are carnivores, with the young eating small invertebrates while older fish extending their diet to include small fish. On calm summer evenings, an explosion of small prey fish on the surface of a lake is often an indication that a hunting shoal of perch is on the move. Perch are cannibalistic and can self-regulate populations should numbers become too high.

Female perch produce sticky bands of eggs, which they wrap around vegetation and rocks. It is thought that these eggs may also have the ability to temporarily adhere to the legs of ducks and other waterfowl, which enables perch to colonise new water bodies. I say 'thought', with a degree of due diligence, because while this is widely assumed to be the case, recent research by the University of Basel has found that there is no definitive recorded evidence that such egg transfer ever happens. That said, there is one reservoir I know in Scotland where perch suddenly materialised out of the blue. This, of course, could have been a human introduction, but equally plausibly, waterfowl were the conduit.

A gravid female perch is so packed full of eggs that she becomes bloated and rotund in appearance. Despite this fecundity, many perch populations in Britain were decimated several decades ago by a virulent disease known as 'ulcer disease', a condition where holes eroded into the lateral body wall of the fish, leading to large scale mortalities. It is estimated that more than 98 per cent of the perch in Lake Windermere were killed by the disease during the warm summer of 1976, although numbers have since bounced back.

I plunged my head under the water several times to observe the fish further until I became distracted by a strange beast that crawled along the bottom: the nymph or larva of a stonefly. For two to four years, these armour-plated mini predators inhabit our lakes, ponds and rivers, and then in a miracle of nature emerge as wing borne flies to mate, lay eggs back in the water to create the next generation and then die. It is the circle of life, which never fails to amaze in its complexity of arrangement yet simplicity in execution.

Head dripping, I decided to call it a day from my impromptu lake dipping and wandered farther along the lakeside path. Great crested grebes and tufted ducks glided out on the water, as did a pair of gadwall ducks. The drake gadwall is especially handsome, and if the sun is shining bright, his greyish plumage transforms into a sparkling, silvery sheen. The drake has a most unusual chuckling, croaking call, sometimes described as a 'cackling quack'. Indeed, the gadwall's scientific name *strepera* arose from a belief that the birds were particularly obstreperous – nomenclature I suspect based more on speculation than fact, but nonetheless, it is a wonderful example of anthropomorphism.

Great crested grebes have a spectacular courtship display where there is much head shaking and rearing up to each other breast to breast. I particularly enjoy the image conjured by the early twentieth-century ornithologist, Thomas Coward, of such behaviour, which he described as being like 'an upright caress', which reflected this endearing reaffirmation of the pair bond.

Soon, the track took me to a stand of hazels, which were being deliberately managed and coppiced to benefit dormice, and nearby there was a wooden nest box that had been especially erected for them. Dormice are among our most endearing mammals, with golden-buff fur and large eyes, and which scamper through the twigs and branches of hazels and other small bushes with the agility of a squirrel.

Frances Pitt recounted in *Wild Animals in Britain* (1938) an instance where she found a dormouse nest, a woven masterpiece in the low branches, which was little bigger than a cricket ball. She wrote:

The nest was a trifle bigger than usual, which made me suspect it to be a breeding nest. I touched a spray of honeysuckle, a rope which wound round the branch which supported the nest, and in an instant a dormouse face was thrust through its side. A yellow-buff furry head, with large lustrous eyes looked in my direction. Again I touched the branch. Out ran the mouse and after it came a second, a third and a fourth dormouse. The party consisted of a mother and three young almost full-grown, but the latter were rather duller in coat-colour than their parent.

Dormouse

It was an enchanting encounter, and one hopes that after the disturbance caused by the inquisitive naturalist, the young dormice quickly returned to the safety of their nest. Dormice are scarce creatures in England and Wales; and absent from Scotland. They are traditionally associated with coppiced woodlands, although recent research has shown they occur in a variety of habitats, including scrub, bramble, coniferous plantations, hedgerows and even the central reservations of dual carriageways – another telling reminder of the importance of our verge sides as a haven for wildlife. Dormice hibernate in winter, and one threat they face due to climate change is awakening from their slumbers during the dead of winter during mild spells, yet when there is still little food about, and which saps precious energy resources.

On my return route at Slapton Ley, a shimmering drift of greater stitchwort and bluebells swept up a steep bank. Blue upon white is a perfect colour combination, so I sat by the edge of this floral splendour for a while to appreciate the beauty of the flowers and to watch the grebes and ducks out on the ley. A Cetti's warbler piped-up behind me, but I had already seen one earlier in the day, and I wasn't going to give this noisy individual the satisfaction of engaging in a fruitless game of hide and seek.

———————————

Chapter 5

DANCING BRIMSTONES & AN ENCOUNTER WITH A MALIGNED SNAKE

April 2022, Somerset Levels

Under the shadow of Glastonbury Tor, glorious April sunshine beamed down upon Shapwick Heath which lies in the heart of the Somerset Levels. It felt as if nature was holding its breath in anticipation of the season of procreation such was the tingling aura of excitement that permeated the air like a seeping mist.

Glastonbury is a place that evokes bewitching visions of Druids and Pagan worship, of mid-summer sunrises and the search for the Holy Grail. It is a place shrouded in myth, folklore and intrigue, and where nature and humanity were once merged in blissful harmony, but which later descended into conflict.

This enveloping aura of mystique ebbs into the very heart of the nearby Shapwick Heath, which is part of the Avalon Marshes and which forms a rich mosaic of meadows, woodland, reed-beds, lakes and pools. Neolithic people lived in the reed swamps, prospering from its natural resources, including abundant waterfowl and fish. These earlier settlers were even resourceful enough to build wooden walkways to help traverse the marshy expanses.

The Romans, too, lived on the edges of the marshes, building villas and farming the higher lands. But the pressure on the landscape grew more intense with each passing century. Since before the Domesday Book, people have been draining the levels for agriculture and the harvesting of peat – although the watery environment never completely succumbed to the murderous onslaught and large tracts of marshy ground still remain, much of which have been actively restored in recent times. A myriad of ditches, rhynes and waterways criss-cross the landscape and despite the trauma of the past, the Avalon Marshes represent one of the finest remaining lowland wetlands in Britain.

On the track ahead of me, a billow of dust puffed up into the air. It was a pair of kestrels, a male and female spread-eagled on the track and using rapid movements of their wings and shuffling of bodies to create a mini sandstorm. Dust bathing is an effective technique to keep feathers in tip-top condition, with dust absorbing excess oils to prevent the plumage from becoming greasy or matted, thus ensuring efficient flight and insulation. Other debris such as parasites are removed as the dust is preened away.

Once the kestrels had finished their dust bathing, they took flight and settled in a nearby hedgerow where they began to chatter busily amongst themselves like a pair of love-struck teenagers. A deep canal-like ditch bordered the edge of the track, and lured by the temptation of water, I followed its course and soon emerged into a stretch of willow and alder carr where brimstone butterflies glided and spiralled in the sunnier, more open parts. Brimstones are exquisite butterflies, the male displaying lovely sulphurous-yellow wings. In the past, the brimstone was known as the 'butter-coloured fly', which lay behind the foundation for the name butterfly that is so ubiquitous today. The brimstone is fussy in its requirements and needs the presence of buckthorn and alder buckthorn upon which its caterpillars are totally reliant for food.

The brimstones at Shapwick were flighty and constantly on the move, but one settled on the ground long enough for me to appreciate its form in greater detail. At rest, the gently scalloped wings were held upright and closed, with a distinctive small brownish circle in the middle, almost like a beauty spot. Brimstones are strong flyers and can move considerable distances in their quest for new habitats to live in. They hibernate and can live for up to a year, which is a long time for such a fragile creature, and by the end of their lives their wings become tattered like flags on storm-tossed boats.

Cast upon the air like a fluttering piece of orange and white confetti, another little butterfly danced and birled close by me. It was an orange-tip butterfly – my first of the year. I followed its progress, but each time it was about to alight on the ground, a new zest for life filled its wings, up and on its way the butterfly soared once more.

Orange-tips are often described as 'feel good' butterflies, and no wonder, because they have a brightness and freshness about them that mirrors a crisply ironed tablecloth. It is the brightness of the tangerine-tipped wings of the males combined with that dazzling whiteness of the rest of the body that sends the spirits soaring, a happy and reinvigorating contrast. The French call the orange-tip 'aurora', representing the glowing sun at daybreak.

The orange-tip was also once known as the 'lady of the woods', but that is a rather inappropriate name because it is more a butterfly of grasslands and hedgerows where it can seek out its favoured plants to lay eggs on such as cuckoo flower and garlic mustard.

I sat for a while by a dark, peaty pool in a thick area of carr where yellow flag iris thrived by the margins. *It was a pity*, I mused, that *I had not brought my snorkel and facemask to peer into the coppery depths of this woodland pool.* Willow and alder carr is a rich habitat where the twisted tangle of roots below the water's surface act as home to a vast array of invertebrates. Bog woodland are honeypots for warblers to find bounteous food, and for bats to twist and weave in search of moths and rising mayflies.

Later that day, I ventured to the nearby RSPB Ham Wall reserve. Unlike the solitude of Shapwick Heath, it was busy with birdwatchers armed to the hilt with telescopes and telephoto lenses and the like. Despite the bustle, this was a place I immediately warmed to. Great white egrets and bitterns haunt the reedbeds, and it is an environment full of wildlife surprises, no more so than when the first scan with my binoculars brought the reward of a glossy ibis wading in the shallows of a mere. The glossy ibis belongs to

Glossy Ibis

the Mediterranean and is a rare visitor to Britain, although numbers are increasing. The winter just past had been extremely dry in Spain, and in Britain it was milder than normal, which encouraged good numbers of these glossy-green and pink wading birds to visit our shores. It is entirely possible if this trend continues that glossy ibis will begin nesting in Britain.

I was especially taken by a group of black-tailed godwits that had settled on a boggy bank in the middle of the mere. Resplendent in their russet breeding plumage and featuring subtly upcurved long bills, they gently slumbered in the sunshine. Small numbers of black-tailed godwits breed in the Ouse Washes and Nene Washes in East Anglia, but the birds at Ham Wall were almost certainly from the Icelandic breeding population and would soon be migrating northwards. A small group of godwits took to the air momentarily, revealing their distinctive black tail bands set against a white background.

Stefan Buczacki, in his *Fauna Britannica* (2002), wrote that the existence of such names as 'yarwhelp' and 'whelpmoo', which imitate the clamorous call that the black-tailed godwit makes when nesting, reveals that it was once a much more common breeding bird in Britain than it is today. Buczacki also noted that, like curlews, godwits were once choice birds for the table and speculated they were cooked underdone 'after the manner of snipe and woodcock'.

Another sweep with the binoculars revealed a little egret, several shovelers, and a drake garganey accompanied by two females. Garganeys are scarce ducks and I could not recall if I had ever seen one before in Britain. They favour fenland and marshes in Norfolk and a few other select areas in the northwest and northeast of England. The drake is an attractive bird, with a dark brown crown, chestnut cheeks and distinctive white facial stripe. Ornithologist, Thomas Coward, in his three-volume *Birds of the British Isles* (1920-5), noted, 'When scared it springs clear of the water with the agility and the velocity of the teal'.

In the distance, a great white egret flew over the reeds, before suddenly spiralling down and disappearing. These impressive white-plumaged herons are another new coloniser, and despite being at an early stage of my British wildlife journey, I was becoming increasingly amazed at the range of birdlife present in southern England, which would have been absent when I was a child. I reeled some species off in my head: little egret and cattle egret, crane, Cetti's warbler and spoonbill came instantly to mind. Whilst climate change is undoubtedly one reason for this foreign invasion, I imagine equally important has been the protection and enhancement of wetland habitats in Britain and northern Europe by conservation organisations such as the RSPB.

It was difficult to draw myself away from the mere because it held so much fascinating birdlife, but a nearby narrow canal aroused my interest. I slowly walked its length, carefully scanning the water. A sinuous movement by the far bank brought a cry of excitement. It was a grass snake, its yellow-collared head poking above the water and its long greenish body rhythmically undulating from side to side as it propelled itself through the water. When I sped up to keep pace with the snake, it hastened to keep a safe distance, and all the while it was continually watching me with keen eyes. This was an intelligent animal, and while it may have been a cold-blooded reptile, there was an underlying warmth to its persona which was most compelling. There was grace and elegance in its movement, slipping through its watery world with the ease of a hand sliding into a well-worn glove.

Many people have an innate fear of snakes, which in the case of the grass snake, is completely baseless as it is a harmless creature that does much good.

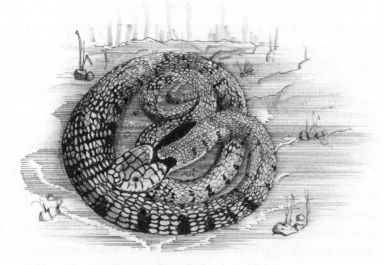

Grass Snake

I enjoy the writings of the early twentieth-century naturalist, Edward Step. In *Animal Life of the British Isles* (1921), he was most indignant over the British press sensationalising stories about snakes to their overall public detriment:

Every summer and autumn our daily newspapers afford evidence that on the subject of snakes the average man has not advanced in knowledge beyond that of his prototype a thousand years or so back. With all that has been done in various ways during the last half-century to spread knowledge of natural things, it is astonishing that editors should admit scare reports about snakes without a line to set the reader right. Internal evidence shows that nine-tenths of these alarming reports about poisonous and aggressive snakes refer to the innocuous grass snake. This is the kind of thing that reflects the vaunted intelligence and calmness of the average Briton.

Grass snakes feed on frogs, toads, newts and small fish; young snakes will also seek out invertebrates, especially worms. At Ham Wall, they also prey upon marsh frogs, which are an introduced species from Europe, and which prosper in its watery shallows. It is likely that marsh frogs are detrimental to native amphibians through competition for food, predating directly upon them and acting as disease vectors for conditions such as amphibian chytrid fungus. Thus, grass snakes play an important role in keeping a check on marsh frog populations at Ham Wall and elsewhere in England.

Once, when searching for terrapins in a ditch in Corfu, I caught a grass snake in my hand and I recall well the inherent power of its body as it writhed furiously in a bid to escape, so much so that I quickly let it go, fearful of inadvertently harming it. Edward Step too had experience of handling these fascinating animals, which he highlighted in his own unequivocal manner:

> When captured the grass snake seldom makes any attempt at biting, though it will hiss freely and snap its jaws. It usually seeks rather to disgust its captor by the voiding of a fetid secretion with a strong odour of garlic among other objectionable scents.

Chapter 6

IN SEARCH OF SAND LIZARDS
& THE MAGIC OF SEAWEED

May 2022, Dorset

The last time I had visited the pretty village of Yetminster in Dorset was as a boy, so perhaps I was naïve in not expecting change. All landscapes transform over time – new houses are built, barns are demolished, small trees grow big and large ones tumble to the ground. Nonetheless, the disorientation was a shock, for the memories were crystal clear yet now everything was clouded. I wandered some more, then ventured down a likely-looking track. The picture frame from the mind slowly took shape. *'Yes, this was the place.'*

Visiting a friend of my mother's in the mid-1970s, and relentlessly bored by adult conversation, I had roamed the countryside by Yetminster to help pass the time and recall watching large bats flying on purposeful wings over the surrounding fields at dusk and glimpsing a diminutive water shrew by the banks of the local stream.

I was so taken by the countryside around Yetminster that I remember vowing to return, and so here I was more than 40 years later. The large bats I had seen back then were serotines or noctules, but I did not have the knowledge at the time to tell them readily apart to make an accurate identification. The water shrew had excited me greatly, its dark-furred body scuttling by the stream edge. A year or two previously, I had found a dead water shrew by a burn that tumbled into Loch Earn in Perthshire, and as I cradled its diminutive velvety body in my young hands, I wished it were possible to glimpse a live one. Thus, it was thrilling that my prayer of hope had come to pass only a relatively short period thereafter by this Dorset brook.

It was wonderful to be back, and the memories cascaded upon my consciousness as if it were yesterday. On a rough path by the stream, I became submerged in a flush of spring wildflowers – garlic mustard and red and white dead nettle, comfrey and mayweed to mention but a few. A pair of little egrets took to the air from a pool in the stream and settled on the bare branches of a dead ash, where they watched me closely. A garishly-plumaged mandarin duck also swept up on fast-beating wings, and peacock and speckled wood butterflies danced and floated in the air.

That evening, I stayed over in the hamlet of the delightfully named Sandford Orcas, near Sherborne, and at dusk walked along a nearby country lane with my bat detector in the hope of spotting a noctule or serotine bat, as I had all these years ago at nearby Yetminster. Electronic bat detectors pick up the ultrasonic calls of bats as they hawk for insects and converts them into sounds that can be heard readily by the human ear and are useful for identifying many types of bats because they call within specific frequency ranges.

It was one of those special spring evenings, with tawny owls hooting and new-born lambs baaing, and the cool air holding the promise of a settled spell of weather to come. The countryside around comprised gently rolling cow pasture, interspersed with hedgerows and copses. It was like being immersed in a little secret corner of England. I adore the softness of dusk, where trees and rounded field outlines gradually merge into one as the light diminishes.

It did not take long for the bat detector to buzz into life and several smallish bats whooshed up and down the lane, making regular passes. The detector picked-up a variety of different call frequencies ranging from 35 to 100 kHz. Those at 55 kHz were most likely to be soprano pipistrelles as that is their peak frequency, whereas the common pipistrelle is lower at 46.5 kHz. As for the higher range frequencies the detector was picking up, they may have been Natterer's bats, which swoop typically at head height in a fast and agile flight. The soprano pipistrelle is so like the common variant that only in recent times has it been differentiated as a distinct species, with the call frequency being the easiest way of telling them apart, although there are a variety of other subtle morphological and ecological differences.

My mind spun into action. *Why two species, when one would do?* It is an interesting enigma, and which reminded me of my son, Ross, asking the very same question when we were in an Alpine meadow – *Why so many species of butterflies pollinating wildflowers when one could do the job just as well?* Butterflies are on the wing at various times in the summer and flowers bloom at different times, so that butterflies will have evolved to specialise in certain plants, both for nectar and for their caterpillars to feed on. Similarly, some plants will themselves adapt to flower at different times to reduce competition for pollinators. Flowerheads may also adopt different shapes that some insects will specialise in. It is all about finding niche advantage.

Pipistrelle Bat

The same applies to the common and soprano pipistrelle. While both take a wide range of insects such as flies and midges, sopranos eat mainly those types associated with water. In other words, the two bats occupy slightly different ecological niches. It is nature being fine-tuned to the tiniest detail and it seems likely sopranos and common pipistrelles were as one in the distant past but have diverged to specialise in marginally different lifestyles.

The following day, I visited the RSPB reserve at Arne, which borders the vast natural sea enclosure of Poole Harbour. The weather was clear and bright, and I turned up early in the hope of spotting scarce sand lizards basking in the sun as they sought to warm themselves up. I scoured a small sandy cliff by the edge of Poole Harbour, which is a favoured breeding site for these colourful lizards, but despite a painstaking search drew a blank. I swept the bank once more, but there was no movement, although in the shallows off the beach, a great crested grebe glided across the water.

I sparked up a conversation with a nearby birdwatcher, who frustratingly had seen a sand lizard only moments earlier, as well as a Dartford warbler. The lizards were about but they are notoriously fickle creatures and, as is always the case when seeking nature, Lady Luck needs to be a constant companion. Due to dramatic habitat loss, the sand lizard is Britain's rarest native lizard and is a specialist of heathland and dune habitats, with a sporadic distribution that includes Dorset, Hampshire, Surrey, West Sussex and on the Lancashire coast at Sefton. Interestingly, there is a long-standing introduced colony on Coll in the Inner Hebrides. Despite the exposed position, Coll is an ideal location for sand lizards, given its mild and surprisingly sunny climate.

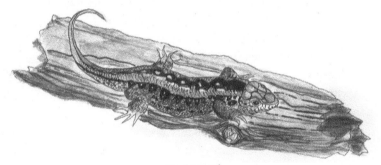

Sand Lizard

Not glimpsing a Dartford warbler was another disappointment as they are one of the star attractions of Arne. They are charming little birds and are heathland specialists that exhibit claret underparts and a longish tail that is often cocked upwards. I recall seeing Dartford warblers in the hills of Les Alpilles in southern France a long time ago, but have never encountered them in England, where numbers are increasing. Like the Cetti's warbler, they are resident warblers and milder winters are probably playing a crucial role in boosting numbers.

I quickly brushed aside the near misses with the sand lizard and Dartford warbler and continued over an expanse of heath until I reached an area of light woodland by a ditch and pond. Sparkling large red damselflies flitted over the path and one alighted by its margin. I crept closer and hunkered down onto my knees to examine it more closely. Here was a marvel of design and colour – with dreamy red eyes, iridescent greenish top-carapace and a long and slender scarlet abdomen, segmented by several, thin black rings. It was the wings, though, that awed, intricately veined so that they appeared like a fine mesh.

A twig cracked nearby and the grass rustled as if brushed by a sudden whirlwind breeze. Slowly rising to my feet, I detected the brown shapes of a pair of sika deer as they slowly moved through the woodland opposite. Introduced from Japan in the nineteenth century, sikas are closely related to native red deer, and many animals in Britain are thought to be hybrids between the two due to interbreeding.

Unlike red deer which often herd, sika tend to be more solitary in their habits. The antlers are also very much smaller than the red. This pair of sika were used to people and tolerated my near presence.

One of the influential books of my childhood was *Mammals of Britain: Their Tracks, Trails and Signs* by M J Lawrence and R W Brown, published in 1967. On sika, the authors wrote: 'The animals are not socially inclined, the stags living alone, and the hinds in groups of two or three except in the breeding season when they too are solitary'.

Another speciality of the heathlands at Arne is the smooth snake, which I anticipated would be even harder to find than sand lizards, so, when I stumbled upon a large piece of discarded corrugated plastic hidden in among gorse, my heart quickened, for I knew there was a possibility a smooth snake could be sheltering beneath. I lifted the sheeting gently, and for a brief second thought I had hit the jackpot when two sinuous forms were revealed, before quickly realising they were slow worms. These coppery, legless lizards are seldom seen, so I was nonetheless delighted by the find, and slowly lowered the sheet back so as not to disturb them.

The twentieth-century naturalist, Maurice Burton, noted that in southern England 'a variety is sometimes seen, known as the blue-spotted slow worm, with blue spots or stripes, sometimes so closely set that the animal appears blue all over'. Slow worms are long-lived animals, with one individual in a zoo surviving for over 50 years.

The sun shone bright and the spring air was warm, and with the recent sight of the calm, silvery water of Poole Harbour, the irresistible urge to don snorkel and mask proved impossible to subdue. I headed a few kilometres west to Kimmeridge Bay and to the Purbeck Marine Wildlife Reserve, which is managed by the Dorset Wildlife Trust. Part of the famous Jurassic Coast, the reserve was established in 1978 and is supported by Smedmore Estate and others.

Kimmeridge Bay is famous for its unique geology, clear seas and diversity of marine life. The black rocks here inspired the name for part of the Earth's history: the Kimmeridgian stage of the Jurassic Period. They were laid down over 150 million years ago on the floor of a tropical sea that teemed with prehistoric marine life.

A long and exposed narrow rock shelf jutted out into the bay, which provided the perfect entry point into the sea. As I slipped in, the scene that unfolded inspired and amazed. This was quite unlike any snorkelling I had experienced in Britain before, with the shallow water exhibiting unusual clarity and a proliferation of colourful seaweeds. One type stood far above the rest for its brassiness – a multi-fronded blue seaweed. Seaweeds are algae, and blue is not a colour one would normally associate with algae or indeed any other plant. This species was rainbow wrack and one which I had never come across before. Bizarrely, if taken out of the water, it immediately turns into a more muted, olive-green seaweed. In Britain, it is found in only the southwest of England and is becoming increasingly scarce, possibly because it is outcompeted by wireweed, an introduced seaweed species from the Pacific, first recorded in British waters in the 1970s.

In a process still not fully understood, the wonderful iridescent blue of the rainbow wrack is produced by a complex process that controls how much light reflects from its cells in a manner that scatters light evenly to all available chloroplasts (the part of the cell involved with photosynthesis or energy production). This may help the seaweed cope with different light levels during high and low tide. This is natural engineering at its most incredible – ingenious, complex, with a resultant beauty that sends the mind spinning with exaltation. Rainbow wrack is also known as magic seaweed – an entirely appropriate name, for this is sorcery of the highest degree.

I flicked my flippers once more and glided over this seaweed paradise. There are over a hundred distinct types of seaweed found in Kimmeridge Bay, including bright-red pepper dulse, sea lettuce and pinkish coralline encrusting seaweeds. It is thought the conditions here are ideal for seaweed because the warm waters from the southwest meet the colder currents from the north, which varies the sea temperatures and gives rise to a bigger variety of species. Furthermore, kelp, which is a large type of seaweed, finds it difficult to gain tenure on the soft underlying clay at Kimmeridge Bay, and its scarcity means plenty of light can filter through to the sea floor to encourage more delicate species to prosper.

Pink encrusting coralline algae abounded, giving added colour and contrast, and one type of seaweed that caught my eye was peacock's tail. This is a strange and distinctive-looking form that looks quite unlike other species. It is cream coloured with lobes, and circular in shape. It was a species I was familiar with from snorkelling in the Mediterranean, and at Kimmeridge Bay, it is right at the northern edge of its distribution. Fish more typically associated with southern climes such as Connemara clingfish and Montagu's blenny also occur here. I was not lucky enough to see either, but corkwing wrasse were abundant, and it was wonderful to watch them sculling through the water with their fast-flickered pectoral fins.

I was reluctant to pull myself out of the water, and after my first attempt, quickly succumbed to the lure of the blazing seaweeds and plunged in once more for a swansong look. Kimmeridge Bay had delivered an underwater experience quite unlike any other, and as I peeled off my face mask for the final time, I knew I had witnessed something truly remarkable.

Chapter 7

THE IMPORTANCE OF DEADWOOD & A DIP INTO ENGLAND'S WATERY 'RAINFOREST'

May 2022, Hampshire

Bright blue skies, still air and vast flat landscape of heath, mere and gnarled trees unfurled before me like a landscape painted upon canvas. This was a place where agile hobbies swoop for dragonflies, woodlarks soar heavenwards and mysterious nightjars hawk for moths, their churring calls breaking the soft, comforting blanket of dusk.

The New Forest is a mosaic environment comprising a variety of habitats, which enhances its wild riches and ensures natural surprises abound at every turn. I had taken a well-trodden track near the bustling town of Lyndhurst and quickly became immersed within the area's hypnotic draw.

The lovely deep call of a stock dove floated across the air from a lone sentinel oak. The bird took to the air in a flurry of wings and glided down to a small peaty pool to drink. Stock doves look like woodpigeons but are

Stock Dove

smaller and more delicate in build. They are easily overlooked, which is a shame, for their plumage has a subtle intricacy that is pleasing to the eye.

Stock dove numbers took a sharp decline in the 1950s and early 1960s due to the impact of organochlorine seed-dressings, but since then, the population has rebounded in many parts of Britain. It is a versatile bird and will nest in holes in cliffs, rocks and trees, and even in rabbit burrows in areas of open ground such as sand-dunes. It commonly nests in tree stumps, or 'stocks', hence the origin of the name.

There is no scientific classification difference between pigeons and doves, for they all belong to the same family, but generally 'dove' is the terminology for the smaller members of the family. It is also a matter of language; the word 'dove', or 'douve' in the twelfth century, has northern European origins, including Old Norse and from the lands that now comprise the Netherlands and Germany, whereas 'pigeon' has French roots. Dove has also become synonymous with gentleness and innocence, which is most appropriate, for the shape of a dove comprises soft lines that hint of an altogether benign provenance.

Like the etymology of the word 'dove', the New Forest derives from an evolution of words. William the Conqueror created it as his new hunting forest in 1079, or 'Nova Foresta'. The word 'forest' refers not to trees but as an area subject to Forest Law, making it an exclusive hunting area for the King and his consorts.

As I wandered deeper into its vast hold, meadow pipits sprung up before me and a lapwing performed a spectacular sky dance by rising into the air in wild abandon and then tumbling to the ground on floppy wings before pulling-up at the last moment. A hobby, newly arrived from its African wintering grounds, flashed across the sky but disappeared before I had a chance to bring my binoculars to bear. They are attractive little falcons, with which I hoped to become more closely acquainted later in my wildlife journey.

There was an abundance of old tumbled tree trunks and I wandered over to a long-deceased oak and ran my hands across its rough bark. The demise of a tree may seem a tragedy, but the reality could not be further from the truth because deadwood forms an incredibly important habitat for wildlife.

Even the most cursory examination of the old and decaying trunk of a fallen tree will reveal the diversity of life that lies within. Peel apart the soft and crumbling bark and inside are a myriad of tunnels created by thriving populations of specialised invertebrates. On the surface of the trunk are intricate tiny cup-shaped lichens, fungi and many different types of mosses, along with the bullet-mark indentations created by foraging woodpeckers.

As well as the sheer diversity of life within deadwood, it also plays an ecologically vital role in carbon capture and in the soil nutrient cycle, slowly releasing nitrogen back into the environment. Deadwood is as vital to the health of a woodland ecosystem as is a living oak with the multitude of species that depend upon it for life.

The simple physical result of a tree or group of trees blowing over provides new diversity in the forest. The clearings created bring dappled sunlight to the woodland floor that encourages wildflowers and other growth, which in turn attracts butterflies and dragonflies and numerous other invertebrates that themselves are preyed-upon by shrews, birds and bats. The fallen seeds of trees germinate and grow in these sunny open places, completing the continuous circle of natural regeneration and delivering new vitality to the woodland.

New Forest Ponies

By a clearing, a small group of New Forest ponies sauntered past, barely giving me a second glance. There are about 5,000 ponies in the New Forest which are wild in the sense that they are free to roam, although they are in reality semi-feral and owned by 'commoners'. This is a tradition that hails back to William the Conqueror where locals were given rights to graze their animals on the 'common', or in this instance, the New Forest. It is their grazing, combined with that of cattle, which has helped sculpt the New Forest landscape of today. Their grazing actions lead to large areas of short-cropped, almost lawn-like grass, which enables wildflowers such as wild gladiolus and chamomile to thrive and leads to open spaces that are perfect for birds such as Dartford warblers and insects like the southern damselfly, which even lays its eggs in the hoof-print puddles created by cows and horses.

Soon, I came to a large shallow, oval-shaped pond where a little egret stalked the muddy edge and a grey heron warily monitored my approach. I did not want to disturb either bird, so I retreated and stopped to admire a clump of round-leaved crowfoot, which flourished in a small puddle. This is a different species from the common water crowfoot I am more familiar with in fast-flowing Scottish rivers and I pondered whether it was able to colonise shallow puddles by being carried on the feet of grazing animals.

Keen to explore other parts of the New Forest, I ventured to Eyeworth Pond by the village of Fritham, a few kilometres northwest of Lyndhurst. Colourful drake mandarin ducks squabbled in the water as they fought for the attention of females and scores of tadpoles swarmed below the surface. A bird photographer stood motionless not too far away, and, at first, I thought he was focusing his camera on the ducks in the water. On approaching close, I realised instead he had placed sunflower seeds on a fence post and was photographing marsh tits and nuthatches which were swooping down to feast upon this bounty.

I struck up a conversation and was most taken by his passion for nature and the patience involved in his photography – an example of where the natural world gives people both enjoyment and relaxation. As we chatted, my eyes were drawn to the marsh tits flicking back and forwards in eager abandon. They are delightful and unassuming birds, with glossy black caps and warm brown upperparts. The marsh tit tends to visit gardens less frequently than other tit species and is a bird that goes about its business largely unnoticed.

During my visit to Hampshire, I was keen to explore the chalk streams and rivers for which the area is renowned, such as those of the Test and the Itchen. Chalk streams are idyllic places with their crystal-clear waters and abundant underwater plant life making them places where one can linger with dreamy abandon for hours on end. They are created when chalk downland produces underwater springs, resulting in surface streams that emerge from the aquifers and which often flow over flinty gravel beds, producing water rich in dissolved minerals. The key features of a typical chalk stream are an alkaline ('hard') water chemistry and a steady flow of clear water at a relatively constant temperature which cushions the ecosystem from summer highs and winter lows. Due to the water having been filtered through the chalk bedrock, it is clear and does not contain the amount of sediment normally found in a stream or river fed by water run-off from the land.

There are fewer than 300 chalk streams in the world and most are in southern England, with a handful in France. They are often referred to as the equivalent of England's rain forests or the Great Barrier Reef, and are found from Yorkshire through East Anglia, the Chilterns, Kent, Hampshire and Dorset. More than 40 chalk streams occur in Dorset and Hampshire, covering the Hampshire Avon and parts of the Dorset Stour and Poole Harbour catchments. If well managed, chalk streams provide sanctuaries for a huge variety of species.

Unsure which one to visit, I opted for a section of the River Test in central Hampshire. The River Test is very much sculpted by the hand of humanity, and as well as the main river, its flow is characterised by a braided channel system that is a legacy of the historic uses of the river for milling for land irrigation of water meadows and for navigation.

Immediately upon arrival on a remote section of bank, I was struck by the beauty of the surrounding meadows and the gin-clear flowing water of the river. A large trout glided over the bottom and grey wagtails hawked for insects by the water's edge. The urge to enter the water was insurmountable, so I stripped off and slipped in with snorkel and mask. Considering the time of year, the water was warmer than anticipated and I gently scrabbled around in the shallows, mindful of the need not to disturb the fragile ecology.

A bed of unbranched bur-reed, their long, straggly, string-like leaves tapering down the water flow, flashed below me, before I swam into a quiet backwater where the water was as still as a pond. Shoals of minnows flickered back and forth. I hung motionless for a while watching their flashing movements. Minnows are one of the bedrocks of our river systems, the fish that supports so much else. Kingfishers and herons eagerly devour them, as do large trout.

In the past, minnows were eaten by people. Izaak Walton, in *The Compleat Angler* of 1653 wrote:

> And in the spring they make of them excellent Minnow-tansies; for being washed well in salt, and their heads and tails cut off, and their guts taken out...being fried with yolk of eggs, the flowers of cowslips and of primroses, and a little tansy; thus used they make a dainty dish of meat.

In 1394, William of Wykeham gave a banquet at Winchester to Richard II, and among the items on the menu were seven gallons of minnow, costing 11*s* 8*d*.

The River Test is home to around a dozen types of fish, including salmon, grayling, bullhead, dace and pike. It is the brown trout for which the river is most famous, and as I swam back into the mid-flow of the river, one torpedoed past below me. These chalk stream trout are much sought after by anglers. Angling is such a satisfying way of getting close to nature and for me blissful happiness is wading in the middle of a river and with a flick of the wrist sending forth the fly-line in a gentle unfurling arc. One becomes part of the river, forming an instant connection with the water's pull around your boots and the constant awareness of the river's power and strength, and its gentler side too. Then the rod bends and the line tightens – a trout has taken! More times than not, it will be a small fish, but the beauty and intensity of pattern inscribed upon these little gems never fails to astound. The brown trout is one of the biggest misnomers of them all – a more appropriate name would be red-speckled trout, or burnished copper trout, or something in that vein, for they are shimmering concoctions of every hue imaginable.

The Test is famous for the quality of its trout angling, although fishing on chalk streams can be a challenge. Terry Lawton in his 2007 book,

Fly Fishing in Rivers and Streams: The Techniques and Tactics of Streamcraft, stated:

> A smooth-surfaced, gin-clear, gentle chalk stream can be very intimidating for the angler. The harmful effects of every bad cast and presentation will be magnified by the water clarity and the smoothness of the surface. Adding to the difficulty will be those monster trout lurking in the shadows and watching everything that is going on, with a contemptuous sneer on their faces.

I veered down a small tributary beck for a short distance where it was so shallow that I crawled along the bottom and the water flow so fast that clouds of bubbles swirled past my facemask. There was a low-cropped and flat-leaved plant on the stream bed here, which I did not have the expertise to identify with certainty, although I suspected it was the early emerging leaves of water crowfoot.

I slithered out from the beck, with small scratches from the gravelly bottom etched upon my belly and sat for a while to let the sun dry my skin and provide time to reflect. Chalk streams are sparkling slivers of unparalleled beauty drawn out from the depths of the bedrock, and which spill forth an abundant and diverse miracle of life from their white-gravelled shallows. They are special places, which face so many threats, including over-zealous water abstraction to meet the needs of southern England's burgeoning population, and which threatens to turn off the tap that supports so much nature. Their conservation and sustainable management are a priority, otherwise England's 'rain forest' could dwindle to a mere shadow of its former self.

Chapter 8

THE RICHES OF THE SOUTH DOWNS
& A VENTURE OF NOSTALGIA

May 2022, Sussex

A rolling vista of chalk downland undulated before me. From the ridge at Harting Down in West Sussex the vastness of England's green and pleasant shires stretched away to the north, while nestled at the bottom of the escarpment lay the little village of South Harting with its attractive church spire piercing the skyline.

Everything about downland is soft and easy, just like the chalk bedrock below, a place of rounded curves, ground-hugging bushes and grazed grasslands where wildflowers and butterflies abound in summer. The landscape is smooth and flowing and pulls you in gently without your senses even aware it is happening.

The South Downs have been inhabited by people since the earliest of times and below my feet on Beacon Hill lay the remains of a late Bronze Age to Iron Age hill fort. As well as the ancient remains, the area of the fort includes an Anglo-Saxon burial mound. Standing upon this site was humbling. *I wondered how many other people from times long past had stood on this very same spot. What were they like and how did they live?* Intriguing questions, most of which we will never know the answers to. In a way, that mystery was appealing; there is something strangely compelling about letting the mind drift and imagine what these distant times were like, rather than having a full and accurate understanding.

Stretching from Hampshire to the white chalk coastal cliffs of East Sussex overlooking the English Channel, the South Downs cover around 1600 km^2 of southern England and are etched deep upon the soul of humanity, even in modern times. In the skies above these domed hills, the RAF and Luftwaffe engaged in dogfights in the dark days of late summer 1940, their vapour trails criss-crossing the sky as people watched horrified below.

After the Norman Conquest, beacons, such as at Beacon Hill, were set up on the Downs to warn of impending invasions from across the English Channel. The presence of settlers harks back much farther than that. My grandfather, Albert Broomfield, who was a farmer on the edge of the South Downs near Brighton, often found flint arrowheads and flesh-scrapers when ploughing the land that were relicts from Neolithic times. When a child, I recall my grandfather gifting me a flint meat scraper and holding it in awe in my hand, my thumb fitting perfectly into its flattened shape, which featured a razor-sharp outer edge. Someone from several thousand years ago had held this object in their hand and now it was grasped in mine. It was a moving and thought-provoking moment that enthralled my young mind.

The stroll along the top of Harting Down was relaxing and my mind continually drifted, which I consciously tried to curtail, for my lack of concentration meant I was missing the nature along the way. I cast my eyes towards the ground where a cluster of cowslips glowed. They were just beginning to flower – but unlike the related primrose – their drooping yellow flowerheads are held aloft on stalks. Cowslips are much scarcer than they used to be, falling victim to the advance of modern agriculture, including the use of herbicides. They are seductive wildflowers which always make me stop in my tracks. The nineteenth-century poet, John Clare, was similarly impressed:

> The dancing Cowslips come in pleasant hours;
> Though seldom sung, they're everybody's flowers:
> They hurry from the world, and leave the cold;
> And all the meadows turn from green to gold.

Sheep farming was the traditional land use of the South Downs and from the Stone Age onwards farmers cleared the trees that covered the hills to graze animals. From early medieval to Elizabethan times, wool was England's main export; and the protracted grazing of the upper slopes over the centuries has sculpted the Downs of today, creating characteristic springy turf grasslands where no artificial fertilisers or pesticides have been applied to the soil, resulting in a rich and diverse flora. The key has been moderation; the grazing by sheep and cattle has been light, which enables wildflowers to prosper and create bee-buzzed meadows.

As I continued my walk, along part of the South Downs Way, white-throats with their rich throaty music sang from stands of blackthorn and skylarks soared heavenwards on trembling wings. A red kite flew overhead with a jackdaw or pigeon grasped firmly in its talons, plucking it in the air and leaving in its wake a stream of feathers that fluttered slowly earthwards in the gentle breeze. Kites are scavengers and I suspected that this meal had been gleaned as a roadkill.

It was too early in the season to see most of the wildflowers and herbs that would adorn these rolling hills in summer, including wild thyme, marjoram, salad burnet, wild basil, small scabious and several types of orchids. Up to 40 different plants grow in just one square metre of chalk downland, which attract many butterflies, bees and other types of insects like grasshoppers and crickets; unusual bee varieties include the blue carpenter bee and the two-coloured mason bee. The latter has a strong preference for chalk downland, especially the south facing slopes. They are attractive little creatures, just over a centimetre long with a black head and thorax, and gingery hairs covering the abdomen.

The two-coloured mason bee is an active pollinator, visiting a wide range of plant species including blackthorn, hawthorn, and gorse, as well as vetches, bugle and violets. This bee has a fascinating life history: it nests in empty snail shells and uses masticated leaves to build several cells for the larvae to develop inside each shell. The snail shell is then camouflaged on the outside with more leaf mastic, grass, dead leaves and old bud scales and pine needles.

Another unusual invertebrate speciality of the South Downs is the rare cheese snail, a diminutive mollusc, so named because of its resemblance to a tiny flat Cheshire cheese. It is found in woodland, especially beech that flanks many of the slopes.

The South Downs overflow with wildlife secrets not immediately obvious to the eye, and I reflected that this would be the perfect place to visit on a warm summer's day and to lie in the short-cropped grass to marvel at the abundance of plants and invertebrates. *How many different species would one glimpse with barely a turn of the head?* Many I imagine and it would be a treasure trove of fascinating life unveiling before one's eyes.

Later that morning, I ventured to Woods Mill, which lies several kilometres north of Shoreham-by-Sea and is a nature reserve managed by the Sussex Wildlife Trust. This was a destination of nostalgia, for I had visited Woods Mill when aged around eight at a time when my interest in nature was fast developing. I was in Sussex visiting my aunt and Woods Mill is indelibly printed upon my mind because a warden at the reserve took me under his wing and showed me the nest of a lesser spotted woodpecker high in the bough of a dead tree at one end of a lake. It was a species I had never seen before and we watched in rapt concentration as the parent woodpeckers, not much bigger than a house sparrow, shuttled to and from the nesting hole.

I recall being presented with a metallic blue and white Sussex Wildlife Trust badge, which I treasured in the same drawer at home which held my flint flesh scraper. As was the case with my recent return visit to Yetminster in Dorset, the passage of time had clouded the memory, and on my arrival, the recollection of the lake at Woods Mill transpired into the reality of a large pond. It was wonderful to be back, however, and with a heart shrouded with emotion, I wandered along the network of paths in the reserve. An enchanting reedy area bordering a nearby smaller pond echoed to a chorus of incredibly loud natural music. This was the song of reed warblers, recently arrived from their African wintering grounds, letting fly their enthusiasm for attracting a mate with true gusto. It was only a small patch of reeds and there must have been no more than three or four males present yet the intensity and volume of the song was astonishing.

The warblers were difficult to see, venting their music from low down in the reeds, but occasionally a bird would sidle up a reed as it sang, revealing its warm brown upperparts and palish breast, before quickly spiralling down again into the hidden depths. Bird reference guidebooks often describe the song as monotonous and disyllabic, and while the latter is true, I found the song uplifting and with no hint of monotony whatsoever. Daniel Greenwood, wrote in his acrostic poem, 'Reed warbler':

Reed warbler song
etched with green daggers,
elongated spears of leaves,
deep in the shadowy murk of
wet stems and skins:
a songburst like a child's
rattle, but just one phrase
breaks into the alder-
leaden air, into willow bows,
extended over a pond fed by the
Regent's Canal.

I was reluctant to leave this reed warbler haven, but eventually pulled away and ambled a slow circuit around the reserve, absorbing its tranquil beauty with my mind whirling with memories. I stopped for a short while to appreciate a wild service tree by the path-edge, its maple-like leaves in the process of unfurling. They are uncommon native trees, usually occurring singly in patches of ancient oak woodland.

Wild service trees grow slowly and their seeds are not prolific in germination; it mainly spreads by suckers. A local name in Sussex and Kent is the chequer tree – one explanation being that the bark peels off in rectangular strips, giving a chequered effect. More likely the derivation stems from the brown fruits, which are said to taste like dates and in the past were brewed into a potent, alcoholic beverage known as 'checkers'. This is reflected in the many pubs and inns in the southeast of England today called 'chequers' – although it is unclear which came first, the name of the fruit or the inns.

The fissured bark was rough to the touch and as I gently ran my hand down the trunk, I reflected upon how this largely forgotten tree species was at one time well known and revered but now largely ignored. Much of humanity has lost its connection with nature, and when that goes, we have lost something very precious indeed.

Chapter 9

IN SEARCH OF MARSH FROGS
& REFLECTIONS ON EVOLUTION

May 2022, Kent

Dungeness on the English Channel coast of Kent is an incongruous place – wild and empty, with vast sweeps of shingle, yet the hand of humanity is all around with the myriad gravel pit pools backdropped by the brooding hulk of the Dungeness B nuclear power station.

Despite nature and the impact of people living cheek by jowl, Dungeness is rich in birds and insects and home to scarce plants and lichens, including the rare Nottingham catchfly, a pinkish-white wildflower with hairy leaves that is heavily scented to attract night-flying insects and moths.

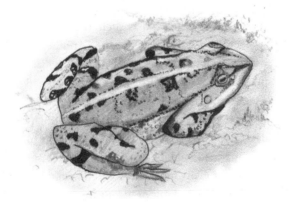

Marsh Frog

I had always yearned to visit Dungeness – not just for the birds, insects or plants, but also for an unusual, introduced amphibian, the marsh frog. As a youngster, I first became aware of their presence in Kent when reading avidly the *Observer's Book of Wild Animals*. Published in 1971, the book stated that marsh frogs thrived on the Romney Marshes, which lie close to Dungeness. The author, Maurice Burton, revealed that they were first introduced into Britain in 1935, when 12 specimens were 'liberated' into a pond on the edge of the marshes. 'Since then, they have penetrated the dykes and canals of the marshes, including the Walland Marsh', he wrote.

In the years that followed, they became so numerous that their croaking at night brought complaints from local residents. It is a frog I am well acquainted with from visits to southern Europe: when exploring ditches in the Mediterranean area, it is not unusual to hear a distinctive 'plop' as a disturbed marsh frog which had been sitting on the bank edge leaps into the water. As for the call, I recall from a visit to Greece that it is indeed loud – a gurgling chorus, with chattering undertones that have been likened to the sound of laughter.

Since its introduction to Kent, the marsh frog has spread to other parts of England, no doubt aided by further releases, and now occurs in Sussex, East Anglia, Somerset, Devon and Cornwall, and the Isle of Wight. It is Europe's largest frog and quite distinctive from our own native common frog, being brighter green in colouration with a distinctive yellow stripe running down the back.

They are striking amphibians, and as such, the draw of Kent's marsh frogs had always held special appeal for me. Another reason for my keenness to venture to Dungeness was the familiarity of its distinctive peninsula that juts out into the English Channel, which had often caught my eye when flying from Scotland to Continental Europe. From the high vantage of an airplane, Dungeness seemed to almost touch Cap Gris-Nez in the Pas de Calais on the French coast. Dungeness is where Britain meets mainland Europe, separated only by a narrow band of silvery sea. Britain might be an island but for many birds and bats, and wind-blown seeds, the Channel is no barrier at all, just a minor inconvenience to passage.

I had picked a good time to visit the RSPB reserve at Dungeness, for bird migration was in full flow and on sweeping my binoculars across a large expanse of freshwater known as Burrowe's Pit, there were many waterfowl out on the lake, including gadwalls, shovelers and great-crested grebes, while cormorants dried their crucifix-like wings from their dead-tree perches. This was a place that overflowed with birdlife and with the inherent capacity to deliver a surprise or two.

A female marsh harrier pursued by a lighter-plumaged male swooped overhead, the pair tumbling in the sky, before descending towards a distant patch of reeds. A lesser whitethroat piped-up its simple yet invigorating rapid-fire song of high-pitched liquid notes. The lesser whitethroat is smaller and neater than its common whitethroat cousin, and the song more musical in quality. The bird briefly appeared on the top of a hedge, its pale throat and grey head clear to the eye, although I was unable to distinguish the darker plumage behind the eyes, which gives the bird a slightly masked appearance.

The wonderful songs of reed warblers – which had so mesmerised me in Sussex – also filled the air and were accompanied by the grating chatter of sedge warblers. The next pool I came to held several black-tailed godwits and a lone greenshank on the far side. There was another wading bird I didn't immediately recognise. My first inclination deemed it a ruff, but on closer examination it turned out to be a spotted redshank, an elegant long-legged bird, larger than the common redshank, and with sooty-black plumage patterned with lighter flecks.

This spotted redshank was on migration and the shallow, water-filled gravel pits provided the perfect stopover as it made its way from its African wintering grounds to breeding areas in northern Norway, Sweden, Finland and Siberia. Like the godwits and greenshank, which were also in transit to northern Europe, this spotted redshank depended upon a series of stepping-stone havens during passage to rest and to forage. On watching the waders against the late afternoon sun, it once again reinforced how national boundaries mean nothing to nature and that conservation efforts need to be co-ordinated and fulfilled on a global basis.

The spotted redshank also brought upon my consciousness deeper, evolutionary matters, because behind its graceful form lay a most interesting creature due to its sexual role reversal. After a brief courtship on the tundra lands of the frozen north, the female lays her eggs and the male takes over the all-consuming task of incubation. The flirty female may then mate with another male (or possibly even more) to produce another clutch, before forming hen flocks with other females and embarking upon their return migration, leaving behind the males with the burden of parenthood. A handful of other bird species do this, such as the dotterel (a small plover) and the red-necked phalarope, which is a small wader with a penchant for swimming.

Spotted Redshank

On initial reflection, this is a clever evolutionary ploy as it means the species can maximise its breeding potential on the harsh and unpredictable lands that lie beyond the Arctic Circle. It is much better for each female to produce two clutches of eggs, rather than one. Indeed, perhaps it is surprising that more birds don't exhibit this behaviour, especially those such as waders, whose chicks hatch open-eyed and covered in down, and don't need as much looking after as baby songbirds require because they are ready to forage under the protective eyes of a parent.

Evolution is a complicated and multi-faceted cocktail, driven largely by environmental pressure and catalysed by the lottery of genetic chance. *What sparked such changes in different breeding behaviour from the norm? Or was this the norm for wading birds but most species had evolved away from it?* Essentially, this is an evolutionary battle between the sexes – the male wants to mate with as many females as possible to pass on his genes, and vice versa for the female. It is a complex balancing act where the needs of maximising the number of young surviving to adulthood are another part of the equation.

After a while, I departed the spotted redshank pool and continued my circuit of the reserve. The pair of marsh harriers reappeared in the sky; the male noticeably smaller than the female. *Why so?* One possible reason is because small prey is more abundant than larger quarry, and the male does more hunting for food when the female is incubating, he is better able to provide her with food. The sparrowhawk exhibits similar sexual dimorphism. It is nature at its most resourceful, a miracle of evolution that reduces competition between the males and females for food within the limited resources of their territory. Thus, the male sparrowhawk specialises in smaller birds such as tits and finches, whereas the female can focus on blackbirds, thrushes and birds up to the size of a woodpigeon.

I soon came upon a small watery ditch where a film of limey-green duckweed clung to the margins. This would be a good place for marsh frogs, I thought, but despite careful searching, there was no sign of any. I wasn't too disappointed, for I knew they were there, and that provided a strange sense of comfort.

Chapter 10

GRACEFUL CRANES & GRAVEL PIT HAVENS

May 2022, Oxfordshire, Gloucestershire & Wiltshire

It might seem an overly dramatic comparison, but this tranquil corner of Oxfordshire reminded me of the Okavango Delta in Botswana, which I have been lucky enough to visit on a couple of occasions. Here, at the RSPB reserve at Otmoor, unfolded a sweeping expanse of grazing marsh, creating a star-spangled landscape of sparkling pools and wet flushes where egrets stalked the shallow water margins and kites soared overhead, just as might happen in Africa.

It was a vista of tranquillity and my mind drifted in quiet contemplation at this beguiling atmosphere of nature at work. A variety of ducks dabbled in the patchwork of ponds and pools, and early-nesting greylag geese showed off their recently hatched grey-fluffed goslings. Such was the irresistible pull of the environs that I did not even bother to bring my binoculars to bear upon the ducks in order to identify them. It was the wholeness of the environment that appealed, rather than narrowing it down to individual species – a direct reflection of the wondrous quality of nature and its complex web of interaction.

It did not take long, however, for the importance of the individual pieces in this natural jigsaw to arouse my interest. I had already become smitten by the song of reed warblers from my recent visits to Sussex and Kent, and now it was a male sedge warbler that was taking centre stage, boldly delivering his chattering music from a nearby ditch, the claws on his feet clinging tenaciously to the stem of a reed. Sedge warblers are often fickle and elusive, but this male was so engrossed with the passion of attracting a mate that he threw all caution to the wind and sang as bold as brass from his exposed perch. As he swivelled his head, his deep orange gape continually flashed like a beacon, a vibrant insight of his inner being and a signal of the vitality of spring. Every so often, the warbler swept up into the air in a fluttering song flight, before quickly descending again.

Nearby, over a green and verdant meadow, a frenzied male lapwing tumbled in his aerial courtship display, sweeping backwards and forwards on crazy and seemingly uncontrolled wings. Up he went, then down again like a swinging yo-yo, crying 'pee-wee, pee-wee' all the while. Another swoop brought him close over my head, the pinion feathers on the wings splayed and quivering, the air thrumming in a soft-buzzed resonance from his sharp changes in direction. It would take a hard-hearted female lapwing not to be impressed by such a swashbuckling display, and I grinned ruefully as the hormone-charged male once more swept back across the flood meadow in a low and haphazard flight.

Lapwings

The call of the lapwing is an evocative herald of spring; the plaintive 'pee-wee' echoing across our wetlands and meadows, the last 'wee' often turning into a more excited 'hoo-wee' as the male performs his rolling aerial dance. The distinctive call lends other commonly used country names for the lapwing such as peewit, peesieweep or numerous variations around that theme.

Peculiarly, for such a beautiful bird, the lapwing has in the past often been associated with deceit. Chaucer was not impressed by the parent lapwing's habit of feigning injury to draw predators away from the nest when he wrote of the 'false lapwynge, ful of treacherye'. It is certainly a bold and protective parent and will dive-bomb any intruder that approaches too close to its nest.

Another noise permeated the air as high above sped a fast-winged speck, flying in broad circles before rapidly plunging towards the ground and rising again. It was a snipe, and on each dive, his spread tail feathers created a noise akin to that of a bleating goat. This sound is traditionally described as 'drumming', but to me, the noise sounds nothing like a drum and is more of a higher pitched winnowing.

The snipe is an intriguing bird, with eyes set well back on the head for good all-round vision and the long bill having a sensory tip, enabling it to feel for prey under the soil. The bill can open only at the tip if so desired. Thus, working like a pair of intricate forceps, it can catch and swallow invertebrates without even needing to withdraw the bill from the ground.

A pair of shovelers dabbled down a water channel, the drake resplendent with his shiny green head, and chestnut flanks. Nature has a glorious inventory of unusual and remarkable designs, and the shovel-shaped bill of the shoveler is one of these, so perfectly adapted for sieving out small plant particles and invertebrates from the water.

A red kite flew low overhead and was immediately met by an eruption of lapwings as they rose into the air and began to relentlessly hound it. The kite seemed surprised by the onslaught and quickly spiralled out of view over a line of distant trees. A cuckoo called – 'coo—koo, coo-koo' – such a soft and haunting call, but one that belies the death-knell for some unlucky soon-to-hatch reed warblers, whose nests will contain the ticking timebomb of a cuckoo's egg. Once hatched, the young cuckoo will push the young reed warblers or unhatched eggs out of the nest, so that it can have the undivided attention of the unwitting foster parents.

A passing birdwatcher excitedly told me that there was a pair of cranes about, which could be observed from a nearby hide. I hurried over and soon had the cranes under the focus of my binoculars. They were elegant and enchanting birds with their soft grey plumaged bodies and long black necks. A distinctive white curved stripe led from the back of the eyes and their heads were capped with a small crimson crown that was barely perceptible. A fallow deer grazed close by, and again an imaginary scene from the Okavango flashed before my eyes, reflecting an image of cranes, storks and antelopes feeding side-by-side in blissful harmony.

Many centuries ago, cranes were a common sight on British wetlands but land drainage and hunting hastened their demise. They were a favoured dish at medieval feasts and it is said that over 100 cranes were served at Henry III's Christmas banquet at York in 1251. Cranes were certainly relatively abundant in the past, as is reflected by place names in England such as Cranborne in Dorset, Cranfield in Bedfordshire and Cranwell in Lincolnshire. A statute of Henry VIII in 1538 specifically protected the eggs of cranes – an edict, in all likelihood, to ensure there were still birds left for the King's own table, rather than any early visionary conservation motive to protect the greater environment.

Common Crane

Following several centuries of extinction in Britain, a small number of cranes from Scandinavia and eastern Europe colonised an area of the Norfolk Broads in 1979, and they have slowly expanded their range ever since, with numbers now approaching around 100 breeding pairs, mainly in eastern England, the Somerset Levels and the Severn Valley, with a small population also establishing itself in northeast Scotland. The key has been the provision and protection of suitable wetland habitat; and the expansion of the crane in Britain has been aided by the establishment of the 'Great Crane Project' in 2010, where conservation organisations joined forces to develop an integrated plan to aid their recovery.

Most breeding cranes are found on protected nature reserves and their future fortunes depend upon the availability of suitable habitat such as peatlands and wetlands, which are continually under threat from drainage and disturbance. Restoring and enhancing such areas will not only benefit cranes but also a wide range of other flora and fauna.

The Otmoor cranes were an exciting discovery and on watching them, I reminisced on previous encounters with cranes in Sweden, and only the year before at Loch of Strathbeg, near Fraserburgh, in northeast Scotland where a marsh harrier had also floated into view. Cranes and marsh harriers in Scotland seemed an unimaginable occurrence when I was a child, but today it is a reality. Amid all the challenges facing Britain's wildlife, there is also much to sing about and celebrate.

After leaving the hide at Otmoor, I encountered a bird watcher by the path edge gazing intently through his telescope at one of the pools beyond. Overcoming innate shyness that occasionally overwhelms and curses me in an unstoppable wave, I asked him what he was looking at. It was a little-ringed plover and he generously let me peer through the scope to examine the bird in more detail. It was a delicate little wader, with the plumage more understated than the much more common and larger ringed plover. At the turn of the twentieth century, little ringed plovers were extremely scarce in Britain, but their liking for breeding in man-made gravel pits in more modern times and on the shores of reservoirs has led to a remarkable resurgence.

The importance of gravel pits for waterfowl and waders was brought home to me later that day when I ventured to the vast expanse of gravel pits, pools and reservoirs that straddles the county borders of Gloucestershire and Wiltshire. Known as the Cotswold Water Park, the area comprises over 140 lakes and wetlands covering around 100 km^2, south of Cirencester. The lakes were created in the second half of the twentieth century by the extraction of glacial limestone gravel, which had eroded from the Cotswold Hills, and which had filled naturally from rivers and streams after workings became exhausted in the early 1970s.

The drive across the Cotswolds towards this area of lakes and pools was a picture-postcard of unfolding beauty and included a brief visit to the quaint village of Bibury, situated on the River Coln, a tributary of the Thames. On arriving at one of the main carparks for the Cotswold Water Park, I was immediately disheartened by the throngs of people, so I drove on for several kilometres before slipping down a narrow lane that was bounded by a flooded gravel pit. This was not a nature reserve or anywhere of special significance, but just a run-of-the-mill gravel pit, which appealed to me because of its normality – and its solitude. I vaulted a gate and walked along a narrow path that ran close to the water, which was bordered by thick hedging. A blackcap sang his hearty song and a great tit was also in full musical flow uttering his simple and repetitive 'teacher, teacher' call. Cowslips glowed like nuggets of gold from the path edge and the enchantment of nature quickly took grip.

Through a gap in the hedge, I glimpsed a dog fox bounding towards me over an area pockmarked with rubble from past industrial workings. He picked his way carefully around the rocks and I froze stock still in the hope of remaining undetected. Unfortunately, a whiff of my scent aroused his senses and he immediately stopped, raising his snout in the air to sample the wind. In a flash of blurry russet, he was gone, leaving behind the memory of his full-brushed tail as he vanished in amongst a maze of boulders.

Above the gravel pit hovered a common tern. It plunged into the water and emerged with a small fish, which judging by its elongated shape was most probably a minnow. Common terns are usually regarded as coastal birds, but in England they have taken to nesting around inland freshwater bodies such as gravel pits and they now breed in many parts of the country, albeit in small numbers and not in the same large colonies as sometimes found by the coast. As the tern hovered once more, I pondered upon the similar changes in fortunes in recent decades for the cranes and little ringed plovers that I had witnessed earlier in the day in Oxfordshire. Humanity has destroyed and taken so much away, but in some instances our activities have created new habitats, such as flooded gravel pits. Whilst this may be an inadvertent consequence of industry, the way these areas are now protected and enhanced as nature sanctuaries is a guiding light for the future.

Herein lies an underpinning fundamental of nature conservation – protect, improve, or create good habitat, then the natural dividends are quickly reaped. If the building blocks for a healthy environment are there, everything else falls into place. Creatures and plants are imprinted to look after themselves and thrive in ecological balance – all they need are the right conditions in which to do so.

Chapter 11

HANDSOME HOBBIES & MYSTERIOUS FEN RAFT SPIDERS

June 2022, Suffolk

A sharp-winged hobby swept across the wide azure sky above Redgrave and Lopham Fen, continually undulating downwards to investigate potential prey such as sand martins and dragonflies gliding low over the reeds, before soaring up again. With the speed of an aerial whippet, the falcon made a wide turn over this Suffolk wetland, its body angled to one side and wings digging deep into the warm air, and flew back the way it came, tumbling over my head and close enough to discern its chestnut thighs and streaked breast.

As this wild spirit of the skies disappeared over a distant line of trees, I exhaled a quiet sigh of satisfaction. For every moment it was in view, I had not drawn a single breath such was my rapt awe of its elevating elegance. Falcons are the racing cars of the bird world – well-proportioned and slender in design, enabling them to speed through the air like piercing arrows. The previous day in nearby Essex, I had admired a male kestrel perched on the skeletal branch of a dead tree. He was impeccable in every way, from the colour of his slate-grey head and tail, to his flawless body form. It was the lines, the sleek body lines that really enthralled – so slim and beautifully balanced, with wings folded over the back in impeccable symmetry. It was as if some architect of nature had crafted the consummate creature.

The summer-visiting hobby is similarly perfect, with its shape and form marginally smaller and more delicate than the kestrel. The shanks stand out like a pair of russet trousers, and along with the moustache stripe that runs down from between the beak and eye, the hobby is a distinctive little falcon. The hobby has also carved out a highly specialised hunting niche, catching dragonflies, chafers and small birds on the wing, especially fast-flying swallows, martins and swifts. The speed and agility required to pluck an agile swallow out of the air defies the imagination, following every twist and turn with daredevil dexterity. The energy consumed to fuel a hunting chase must border on the life threatening, and there is little room for error, with a sequence of failed hunting attempts wreaking a terrible toll that saps precious body resources.

The flight of the hobby is more muscular than the kestrel and in some ways is akin to a swift. Indeed, when hunting, hobbies typically sweep their wings back to mirror their avian prey, mimicking their appearance and enabling them to approach close without being detected.

Hobby is an appealing yet unusual name. It most probably derives from an old French word meaning to 'jump about' in reference to the hobby's energetic and agile flight when chasing prey. The scientific name is *Falco subbuteo*, and in the late 1940s when the Great Britain Patent Office refused keen ornithologist, Peter Adolph, to patent a new football board game as 'The Hobby', he instead successfully patented the game as the now famous 'Subbuteo'.

Redgrave and Lopham Fen is Britain's largest remaining valley fen and is a wonderfully wild haven of sedge, rush, heath and pools. It is the source of the River Waveney that forms the border between Suffolk and Norfolk (which spills out into the sea at Great Yarmouth), and of the Little Ouse which flows the other way towards the Wash.

Valley fens are unique places that depend on low nutrient alkaline water that well up from chalk aquifers and springs. Deep peat deposits that built up over thousands of years on the valley floor support rich plant communities ranging from sedge beds to wet heaths.

A major restoration project completed in 2002 saved Redgrave and Lopham Fen from drying out, resulting in many wetland species formerly lost now reappearing. The open expanses of the fen, combined with adjacent woodland, make it a sublime environment for hobbies and a host of other creatures and plants.

One speciality is the rare fen raft spider, which as well as at Redgrave and Lopham Fen, was previously only found on the Pevensey Levels in Sussex and in an area near Swansea. It is Britain's largest arachnid and a cunning ambush hunter, which sits on emergent vegetation with its forelegs resting on the water surface to detect vibrations caused by potential prey. With a span (including legs) of 70 mm, the fen raft spider is a formidable creature that feasts upon invertebrates, and on occasion will even take small fish and amphibians. A spider that can catch and eat vertebrates is a remarkable part of Britain's natural inventory and underlines the surprising diversity of life found upon our shores.

Fen Raft Spider

To boost their fortunes, fen raft spiders were introduced to other suitable sites in the Norfolk and Suffolk Broads between 2010 and 2015, and they are slowly spreading through the Yare and Waveney Valleys. Keen to see one, I carefully scanned my binoculars across the vegetated margins of a pool they were known to haunt. Despite several sweeps, the spiders remained elusive. Instead, my imagination spun into overdrive, conjuring an image of one rapidly gliding across the water like a giant pond skater and delivering its venomous *coup de grâce* upon some unfortunate froglet. My dreamy reverie was quickly brought to an abrupt halt by a fluttering large red damselfly, which spurred me to continue my circuit of the reserve, accompanied by the backdrop of the weak song of a hidden reed bunting.

In a meadow clearing, I caught a momentary back-end glimpse of a small dog-like animal, brown-furred and fleet-of-foot. It was gone in a flash and initially I was not sure what the creature was. On resuming my walk, I racked my brains, and it dawned on me that the beast was almost certainly a Reeves' muntjac, a small deer native to China. They were first introduced in Woburn Park in Bedfordshire at the beginning of the twentieth century and are now widespread throughout much of England and Wales. During my travels in southern England, I had seen muntjac roadkill bodies on several occasions and had already deduced they were widespread. Nearly a quarter of recorded deer road casualties in England are muntjacs and they

Muntjac Deer

undoubtedly compete with native roe deer. Where common, muntjacs impact upon the diversity of woodland flora and threaten the survival of vulnerable plant species such as the oxlip.

The RSPB reserve of Minsmere, on the Suffolk coast, is a gold standard destination for birdwatchers, and later that morning the temptation to explore its environs proved too strong to resist. This was a bird paradise and I spent a productive couple of hours watching avocets and shelducks wading in the shallow pools. A bittern even put in a cameo appearance, its warm-brown head poking up momentarily through thick reeds before quickly ducking down again.

Although Minsmere was enjoyable, I was keen to explore other nearby areas away from this ornithological honeypot attraction, so ventured several kilometres north to the attractive village of Walberswick, from where I struck southwards down a long shingle beach, which was bounded by a natural sea wall, beyond which lay a vast expanse of marsh, pools and sweeping reedbeds. On the upper beach, yellow-horned poppies, sea-holly, restharrow and sea kale prospered.

The yellow-horned poppy boasts a most attractive blousy yellow flower. Whilst the plant has medicinal uses from the past, it is said to be poisonous to consume and can affect the brain. A tale from the late 1600s recounted the plight of a man who had made a pie from the poppy roots, believing they belonged to sea holly. After eating the pie, he became delirious and believed that his white porcelain chamber pot was solid gold and that he was now in possession of huge riches.

Sea Kale

Sea kale is a plant I was unfamiliar with and had never found before. It sports elongated crinkly leaves and in the past was much revered as a delicacy, especially the young shoots which were eagerly sought out. Such was the high demand that sea kale was even gathered for the export market. Inevitably, the culinary popularity and unsustainable harvesting hastened its decline and nowadays sea kale is a scarce coastal plant.

On my return route, I wandered along a path that took me away from the shore and through Dingle Marsh. Nearby lay the 180-hectare Westwood Marshes, which forms the largest single block of freshwater reeds in Britain. The marshes were reclaimed to form grazing meadows in the eighteenth century, but like Minsmere a few kilometres farther south, were flooded in the Second World War for defence purposes and reverted to marshland. This was a watery sanctuary of nature, eternally captivating and with every season unveiling special surprises. In winter, the nearby Blyth Estuary holds good numbers of wading birds such as black-tailed godwits and avocets, while for me, the summer joy lay in the unusual and specialised plants that I had just discovered on the upper shore.

Walking this wild part of the Suffolk coast sent my consciousness meandering in wild contemplation, but one corner of my mind was still raptly focused on the surrounding reeds for any bird movement, especially for scarce bearded tits. I scrutinised every small bird that flitted through the reeds in the hope one might be a bearded tit, but they all turned out to be reed buntings or sedge warblers. I mentally reprimanded myself – all birds are special whether common or rare, and that is a fundamental of nature I had temporarily forgotten. A handsome cock reed bunting alighted atop a swaying reed stem, and to assuage my guilt, I took the time to appreciate the subtle beauty of his sparrow-like body and coal black head. If reed buntings were rare, hordes of twitchers would avidly seek them out, but because they are ubiquitous, they often barely attract a second glance. That is a pity, for every lifeform should be treated as a treasured gem, unique and special, and a vital element of the greater natural whole.

Chapter 12

DANCING DAMSELFLIES & AN UNDERWATER
PEACOCK

June 2022, Norfolk

Dazzling blue damselflies and dragonflies flitted over the clear and enticing water of a sparkling pool at Surlingham Broad, close to the River Yare in Norfolk. This was a shimmering sanctum of calmness, a wild refuge surrounded by reeds where not a breath of wind whispered and the sun shone down bright.

Situated a few kilometres east of Norwich, this broad was a place to linger and let nature come to you, with every moment proving as enticing as the next, the mind engrossed by insects buzzing by and the busy songs of warblers drifting through the reeds. The damselflies were common blues, such beautiful and slender insects with their azure bodies and delicate wings. Initially, I identified the dragonflies as black-tailed skimmers, a type I was unfamiliar with, and which are most striking with their robust powderpuff blue abdomens, tipped with black. But closer examination made me think again, with the dawning recognition that they were instead scarce chaser dragonflies, which as the name suggests are scarce, although this part of Norfolk is one of their strongholds.

As is often my eccentric habit, even when walking in the countryside, I was carrying a snorkel and facemask in my backpack, and with the lure of the pool proving irresistible, stripped off my shirt and gently submerged my face and upper body below its languid surface. The water was surprisingly clear, albeit a little cold, and because only my head and torso were under the water, there was little danger of stirring the bottom and creating billowing clouds of murky sediment. I steadied my breathing and looked around. A small six-legged beast with a flattened body scuttled along the bottom, which resembled some prehistoric beast spirited from the dawn of time. This was a dragonfly larva, a fierce predator that prowls the shallows of these Norfolk pools and ditches for two or three years.

When it is ready to emerge, the larva will climb out of the water and the adult bursts forth as a vibrant full-blown winged beauty. This dragonfly larva brought back recent memories from my head-dunk at Slapton Ley in Devon, where I had encountered a stonefly nymph, which was similar in appearance, although smaller in size.

There were numerous cased caddisfly larvae working their way slowly over the detritus of the pool bed, using tiny particles of grit and vegetation to create a protective tube-like exterior casing. This creates the perfect camouflage from prowling roach and trout, or a kingfisher perched on a branch above, with the rough outer casing acting as a deterrent from being swallowed by fish and birds.

I swivelled my head to one side and caught sight of a great ramshorn water snail. The animal had a large and dark spiralled shell, and gently grazed on a frond of feather-leaved water weed. The weed looked like hornwort and in among its finely divided leaves were a multitude of other tiny snails, while in the water column hung tiny planktonic daphnia (a type of water flea). This was a magically-rich environment that was home to many distinct types of creatures and plants. After a while, I lifted my sodden head out of the pool and sat on a bed of flattened reeds, letting the warm air dry my hair.

On doing so, another damselfly fluttered by on dark paddle-shaped wings, the body an iridescent and gleaming metallic green satin that bordered on blue. It was a banded demoiselle, which must rank as one of

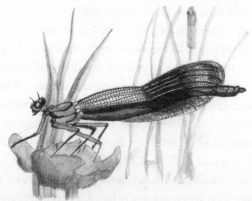

Banded Demoiselle Damselfly

our most beautiful insects. The banded demoiselle is sometimes known as the 'kingfisher', presumably in reflection of its dazzling colour, or the 'water butterfly', which is no doubt a reference to its fluttering flight and burnished tones.

This banded demoiselle was a shy creature, and on carefully taking to my feet to follow its bouncing flight, it showed reluctance to alight anywhere for a rest. Then, another one appeared which finally settled on a reed, enabling me to examine it in greater detail. The vibrant colour was even more striking when seen up close; especially appreciable were the purple legs, which delivered another sparkling colour addition to the overall shining tapestry of brilliance.

Within these first few hours of exploration, I had become enraptured by the allure of the Norfolk Broads and was overcome by an overriding desire to see more. Broad is a Norfolk term for a shallow lake, and the Norfolk Broads is one of Britain's great natural reservoirs of life, a mosaic patchwork of rivers, lakes, fens, ditches, ponds and pools, with sweeping expanses of reeds and scattered woodland. It is an internationally important area for diversity, where rare species abound and the unexpected is always within the realms of possibility.

On leaving Surlingham Broad, I walked along a country lane to Wheatfen, a lush watery nature reserve that is managed by the Ted Ellis Trust. The area of the fen was once the home of Ted Ellis, a writer and broadcaster and one of Britain's great naturalists. The establishment of the Trust after his death in 1987 has ensured the protection and enhancement of the fen, resulting in it becoming one of the most significant and well-studied wetland nature reserves in Britain. Covering 52 hectares, it comprises areas of open fen, reed beds, sallow carr and two small broads. For a visitor to the reserve, the huge attraction is its accessibility, with boardwalks and paths ensuring it is possible to venture deep within its wild bounds.

I meandered through the reserve, following no particular route and taking random turns, revelling in the quiet solitude that was only broken by the calls of cuckoos and the now familiar songs of reed warblers. In a ditch by one of the path edges, a male stickleback flickered in the water below, his red throat and belly briefly glinting in the sun. The male stickleback is the equivalent of an underwater peacock, performing a dashing, zig-zag courtship display to entice a female into his specially constructed nest comprising tiny particles of vegetation glued together with secretions made by his kidneys. Once a female has laid her eggs, she is driven off, and the male guards the nest, fanning water over the eggs with his fins to keep them well oxygenated. Once hatched, the devoted male will defend the fry for a few days, until they are strong enough to go their own way.

I speculated on what other fish haunted the ditches, pools and broads here. Almost certainly there would be bream, rudd, roach, perch, carp and pike, and no doubt others such as tench and ruffe. As I contemplated fish, a damselfly fluttered past and landed on a leaf. It was a willow emerald damselfly, an elegant beauty with a shiny, metallic green abdomen and delicate wings, each one tipped with a white spot. Female willow emeralds lay their eggs on willows and alders that overhang water. It is an intriguing damselfly and a new arrival to our shores having been first recorded in East Anglia in 2007. Since then, it has rapidly expanded its range and can now be found as far north as North Yorkshire and as far west as Warwickshire. As I had already discovered with the Cetti's warbler, the forces of climate change are omnipresent, and over the coming decades many more species will most likely colonise Britain from the Continent, whereas others will become scarcer or may even disappear altogether. Of course, this is nature responding to circumstance, and some species are much better at adapting than others, resulting in winners and losers. While many of the new arrivals to our shores are welcome, the loss of species that were previously native is a tragedy, creating a double-edged sword for which humanity is doing little to abate. I fear the tide is now unstoppable.

Wheatfen is home to an array of other rare and fascinating insects including swallowtail and silver-washed fritillary butterflies, and northern hawker dragonflies. Wildflower specialities include the marsh pea, a specimen of which I found during my wanderings, which exhibited intricate lilac-pink flowers. It used to be scarce at Wheatfen, but a carefully controlled mowing regime on grassy areas has enabled it to thrive in recent times.

My random course through Wheatfen resulted in a loss of bearings, and on my return journey to the reserve entrance, I took several wrong turns and became temporarily lost. This proved fortunate because in one of the ditches I noticed a smooth newt lying on its muddy bottom, its small lizard-shaped body silhouetted against a mostly decayed, but rather pale leaf. I overcame the boyish temptation to scoop it out of the water with cupped hands and instead let it rest in peace. It did, however, spark a childhood memory of catching a pair of smooth newts in a pond on a golf course on the south side of Edinburgh. My friend who was with me at the time, kept them in an aquarium for several days before releasing them back into the pond from which they came. The beauty of the male newt still sticks in my mind, with his velvet grey-blue back, shallow-ridged crest and vibrant orange underparts. Another friend of mine kept palmate newts in a fish tank, and they were voracious feeders, often snapping up small pieces of raw chicken that were dropped into the water. In small hill pools and ditches in Scotland, palmate newts eagerly devour small frog tadpoles, and frogs frequently choose spawning places where newts are absent.

That evening, I settled by the edge of a barley field near the village of Surlingham. As the diminishing soft light of dusk descended, noctule bats began to patrol the treetops on the far margin. They swept backwards and forwards high in the air four or five times, before rapidly tumbling earthwards, where I imagine they resumed their foraging along the field edge lower down.

Several jackdaws and carrion crows had gathered on a large dead oak in the middle of the field, and they seemed to be using its bare branches as a place to relax and socialise after a busy day searching for food and looking after young. As the dark veil of night took grip, they flew off one by one to their nearby roosts, leaving behind the gentle rustling sound of the barley as it was ruffled by the warm nocturnal breeze.

The following day, I strolled along another lane which took me to Church Marsh, a small RSPB reserve, where a female gadwall and her ducklings dabbled in the shallows of a large pool, and where more banded demoiselles fluttered by on their characteristically floppy wings. A comma butterfly flashed past and landed on a willow leaf, displaying its patterned orange, scalloped wings.

Comma Butterfly

The comma is a distinctive butterfly with ragged wing edges and a little white comma mark on the dark underwings, which gives the creature its name. When the wings open this is an insect of stunning colour, but on closure the butterfly almost disappears, the jagged outline of the wings resembling a dull withered leaf amidst the tangle of branches and twigs.

The caterpillar of the comma butterfly takes such camouflage abilities to an even more ingenious level by resembling a bird dropping. Presumably, the forces of evolution have deliberately conspired to make the caterpillar look like bird excrement, which provides a mind-numbing insight into the ingenuity of nature and raises the questions about how this happens and the processes involved. We will never know and can only guess and hypothesise. The only conclusion of which I am certain is that nature is incredible in shape, diversity and form. Despite my practical scientific brain, the mechanisms which deliver such variety inevitably makes me wonder on occasion whether there is a higher being.

Chapter 13

CHARISMATIC CHOUGHS & A CURIOUS SEAL

June 2022, Pembrokeshire

As I stood upon the dramatic coast of the Marloes Peninsula in Pembroke-shire, it felt as if I has been spirited to the portals of heaven such was the unrequited seamlessness of the towering cliffs, stacks, arches and froth-spumed skerries.

Choughs, Marloes Peninsula

There is something gloriously addictive about any coastline, a meeting place between two different worlds and that narrow blurred bit inbetween where both sea and land creatures exist. If I am absent from the coast for any length of time, a deep hankering engulfs my body like a thirst that needs instant quenching. The sea is irresistible in every imaginable way, powerful and seductive like a magical siren call.

A strange, high-pitched cry whirled across the sea breeze – similar to a jackdaw, but with the twanging resonance of an electric guitar string being plucked. Then, two crow-like birds tumbled over this Welsh clifftop on erratic wings and alighted on a grassy slope, their curved scarlet beaks glinting in the morning sun. Choughs!

There are only about 400 pairs of these scarce crows in Britain, with the remote peninsulas and headlands of Wales one of their strongholds. Choughs are incredibly charismatic birds, full of the zest for life and continually calling to one another as if they enjoy the perpetual sound of their own chatter.

The choughs busied themselves on the grass slope, with little puffs of dust flung in the air as they probed the ground with their distinctive long beaks for leatherjackets, worms and other invertebrates. It was a charming sight, and I soon became immersed in their world, with the briny air and colourful drifts of clifftop flowers merging as one ethereal entity.

Chough

Watching the choughs gave me the opportunity to mull over their precarious status. A couple of hundred years ago, choughs were far more widespread in British coastal areas, but their range has since contracted markedly, fuelled by human persecution in the nineteenth century, including from egg collectors.

The other principal driver for decline is due to their fussy environmental requirements of preferring coastlines with swards of short, grazed grass, with nearby beaches for foraging sandhoppers and the like. Choughs do best where low-density livestock grazing occurs close to suitable nesting sites on rock faces, caves and old buildings. Choughs also require places with very mild winters and warm summers, given their need for a year-round supply of invertebrates.

I observed the choughs for a bit longer, until they took to the air in a swirling tumble and veered around a rocky bluff. With the choughs gone, I began to examine the wildflowers on the clifftop. One eye-catcher was common centaury, with delicate lilac petals, centred by a golden orb. This was a dwarf form of centaury, specially adapted to cope with persistent coastal winds.

Sheep's-bit with its purple pincushion-like flowerhead was another plant that brought me under its thrall. Sheep's-bit looks like Devil's-bit scabious, which is so common on northern hills and grasslands in late summer but has a softer subtlety that is most compelling. On one sheep's-bit flower, a spectacular six-spot burnet moth with burnished black and red wings had settled and was eagerly supping the life-enhancing nectar. In nearby rock crevices, sprawling English stonecrop prospered, with the waxy leaves reddish in hue and the small delicate white flowers tinged with pink.

Common Centaury

I gazed out to sea towards the nearby islands of Skomer, Middleholm, Skokholm and Gateholm, and then farther beyond to Grassholm some 13 km away. Grassholm looked snow-capped, but this glaring reflection was in fact guano (bird droppings) from the many thousands of gannets which nest on its shallowly inclined rock slopes. Only the huge gannet colonies on the Bass Rock and St Kilda in

Scotland supersede Grassholm in the number of breeding pairs present.

Puffins breed on Skomer and Skokholm, but the more secretive stars of these two islands are the huge numbers of nesting Manx shearwaters (which also breed on Middleholm). A census in 2018 revealed that there were almost half-a-million breeding pairs on these islands, which equates to well over half the world population of Manx shearwaters. To the north of Marloes, across the vast shimmering expanse of St Bride's Bay lies Ramsey Island, where following a rat eradication programme, the population of breeding shearwaters rose to 6,225 pairs in 2022 – a 30 per cent increase compared to 2016.

When researching my previous book, *A Scottish Wildlife Odyssey*, I wrote about Manx shearwaters on the Isle of Rum. I recounted that on this inner Hebridean island shearwaters breed on four mountain tops, the names of which are Norse in origin. One of them, Trollval, is possibly so-called because the Vikings believed there to be trolls living under the soil – which were in fact shearwaters in their burrows making their strange, haunting calls. Ever since, I have always regarded Manx shearwaters as 'flying sea trolls' – a term of affection rather than the true derogatory meaning for troll. Shearwaters are mystical, and troll is a good encapsulation of this intrigue – underground nesters with superb navigational prowess and which roam huge distances over the ocean during their lives.

This corner of southwest Wales is one of the most important areas in the world for breeding seabirds, attracted by the rich feeding and remote islands to nest on. The islands act like a magnet because they are few and far between in the Irish and Celtic Seas, which means nesting sea birds avidly seek them out.

The draw of the coast was overwhelming and the following day I visited Strumble Head, which lies a few kilometres west of the ferry port of Fishguard. The area is known as the Pencaer Peninsula (although it is not a peninsula) and the focal point is Strumble Lighthouse, which gains foothold on a tiny island just offshore that is reached by a suspension bridge.

Nearby, lies the rocky shores of Carreg Wastad where the last ever invasion of Britain took place in 1796. Four French vessels landed 1,400 soldiers and their subsequent surrender two days later was attributed to their poor discipline and morale; many had become drunk on stolen alcohol. Local people rose to the challenge to resist the invaders, including Jemima Nicholas who, armed only with a pitchfork, rounded up a dozen single-handedly.

Intrigued by the story and what the French landing place looked like, I headed towards Carreg Wastad, where I spotted a pair of choughs wheeling in the distance on black-cloaked wings. I followed their progress around a small headland before hunkering down on a grassy slope to watch them feed by the margins of a small pebbly beach. A grey seal bobbed in the water offshore, and curiosity aroused, it swam in my direction before stopping and eyeballing me from a reasonably close distance. Curiosity is an innate trait of grey seals and this one reminded me of previous encounters with seals on the west coast of Scotland. Take a small rowing boat or dinghy and when sculling around the small rocky creeks and inlets of a sea loch and it is only a matter of time before one is joined by an inquisitive grey seal, its head bobbing in your wake before submerging. You row on and a minute or two later it pops up again, still following the diminishing ripples but always keeping a safe distance. What is it thinking? Why is it so fascinated by the small boat and its occupant? Only the seal knows that. Perhaps it is solely curiousness, or maybe the disturbance of the splashing oars causes fish to dart and reveal themselves from their hiding places in the shallow kelp beds. But whatever the reason, it is just one facet of seals' behaviour that makes them one of our most interesting animals.

The seal by this rocky Pembrokeshire bay soon tired of my presence and headed farther out to sea. I turned on my heels and headed back to Strumble Head, and then followed the coastal path farther to the west. A cock linnet whirled up into the air before settling on the top of a gorse. Linnets love nesting within the prickly protective confines of gorse, or furze, which has resulted in some old country names for the bird that includes furze linnet and gorse thatcher.

Linnets are perpetually shy little finches that are always on the move, but this one stayed still enough for me to appreciate its warm chestnut brown back and greyish head crowned with crimson. Walter de La Mare in his poem 'The Linnet' wrote:

Upon this leafy bush
With thorns and roses in it,
Flutters a thing of light,
A twittering Linnet.

And all the throbbing world
Of dew and sun and air
By this small parcel of life
Is made more fair.

The linnet soon took to the air in an undulating flight to perch on the top of another gorse bush some distance away. The familiar guitar-twang calls of choughs lifted across the air once more, and a pair of these wind-blown crows hurtled past me in a wonderfully random flight. Their calls had an entrancing yet simple quality, and as they landed upon a nearby clifftop, I wondered what the future held for these inherently vulnerable birds.

Linnet

Chapter 14

MUSINGS ON BRAMBLES & 'AERIAL FLOWERS'

June 2022, Carmarthenshire

The white flowers that bedecked this prickly bramble in Ffynone and Cilgwyn Woodlands were larger than normal and belonged to a variety I was unfamiliar with. I had noticed these large-flowering brambles, or blackberries as they are commonly known, by a nearby road verge the previous day, the five petals spaced farther apart and less bunched than usual.

This part of Wales on the border of Pembrokeshire and Carmarthenshire appeared to be a large-flowering bramble hotspot and discovering them brought the opportunity to ponder upon one of Britain's most diverse plants, there being hundreds of different varieties in Britain with subtle differences, including the taste, size and fruiting time of the berries. Indeed, it was entirely possible that the bramble in this Welsh woodland was the Armenian bramble, an introduced type that is more robust than native varieties.

Bramble Flower

Not only do brambles provide fruit in autumn and sweet nectar for insects from their flowers in spring and early summer, but the protective prickly cover of their stems also provides crucial nesting places for birds such as thrushes and whitethroats. Wood mice often use old blackbird nests as feeding platforms in which to devour brambles, and I recall once inadvertently disturbing one, which shot out of the nest in a blurry-brown blur to seek shelter on the ground.

Archibald Thorburn in *A Naturalist's Sketch Book*, published in 1919, described wood mice as being 'easily tamed and pretty creatures to watch in confinement, always keeping their fur in spotless condition, and spending a good part of their time cleaning it'. We tend to think of rodents as dirty creatures but as Thorburn observed, they are indeed fastidious animals that regularly groom and clean themselves.

My initial bramble musings had effortlessly transformed into thoughts about wood mice, such is the way that nature is interlinked to a form a greater entity, with each part dependent upon another. I snapped out of this reflective contemplation and wandered farther along a well-maintained track in Ffynone and Cilgwyn Woodlands. It was an enticing mixed woodland, comprising oak, elm, alder, birch, sweet chestnut, holly, hazel, beech and many other types of tree.

Blackcaps and chiffchaffs sang from the clearings and a spotted flycatcher swooped up from its lookout perch to snatch a tiny fly out of the air. A garden warbler began to sing and I soon detected the elusive songster as it slipped through a tangle of hazel. The fluty song is similar to the blackcap, though more mellow with softer undertones. It is one of our most secretive birds, a relatively frequent summer visitor, yet preferring to keep under cover where its undistinguished brown plumage aids in its perennial concealment.

Herb-Robert, speedwell and white clover brought colour to the track edges and the buzz of bees delivered a constant hum of unbridled contentment. Despite this, I felt a tinge of melancholy, for it was now the middle of June and a feeling of closure permeated the air where the birds will soon stop singing and the flowers drop their petals. I was experiencing the woodland's last joyous breath of procreation and it was a swansong of overwhelming sadness.

In some of the clearings, rosebay willowherb thrived, its tall, pink-flowering spikes pointing heavenwards as if in celebration of this time of warmth and sunshine. Rosebay willowherb is such a tranquil name for a plant, although it is sometimes more prosaically known as fireweed because of its prolificacy in colonising areas of forest destroyed by fire.

I halted in my tracks to immerse myself in this sea of pinkness, watching bumblebees and hoverflies making good the richness of the nectar. Fireweed – yes, a most appropriate name, for these wind-whispered flowers could also be likened to flickering flames. Rosebay willowherb was also once known as bomb-weed because of the speed it occupied city areas laid waste by Luftwaffe air raids in the Second World War.

It is hard to imagine that up until the 1800s rosebay willowherb was scarce in the countryside, but it has since undergone a remarkable spread and is now ubiquitous. The development of railway lines and roads, along with their associated embankments, provided the perfect conduit for willowherb to colonise new areas, aided by those white-fluffed parachute-like seeds that carry far in the wind.

Rosebay willowherb is the supreme opportunist, a pioneer species, with its tall growth enabling it to shade-out plant competitors, thus quickly reinforcing newly occupied bridgeheads, especially in areas of cleared urban land, or recently felled forestry plantations.

Foxgloves also prospered in the more open parts of Ffynone and Cilgwyn Woods, another avid coloniser of such areas, although not nearly as prolific as rosebay willowherb. Foxgloves produce thousands of tiny seeds held in egg-shaped capsules which are scattered a reasonable distance whenever the long-stemmed flowers sway in the wind, throwing them into the air as if launched from some medieval siege trebuchet.

The foxglove is a brassy plant, so eye-catching and dominant compared to our other native flowers, their beautiful purple bell-shaped blooms held aloft on towering spikes. Bumble bees adore foxgloves and I stopped to watch their fur-buzzed bodies enter the tubular flowers before slowly backing out again after having supped their fill of nectar.

Foxglove

Not far from the wood lay a small, enclosed area of sloping grassland. It was not grazed in the fashion that a true meadow might be, but, nonetheless, it was a wonderful place for wildflowers and pollinating insects. Ragged robin thrived in the damper margins, red clover was abundant and drifts of marsh-bedstraw and buttercups swept up the slopes.

I crouched down to examine the marsh bedstraw in more detail, the tiny white flowers delivering a powderpuff effect. It was a straggly plant that utilised the surrounding long grass as a means of support for its own spindly stems, much in the same way as greater stitchwort does. Nearby, a cluster of the related yellow-flowering lady's bedstraw brought colour and contrast to this part of the grassland. The scientific family name for bedstraws – *Gallium* – comes from the Greek word for milk and refers to the flowers of lady's bedstraw which were used to curdle milk in northern England when making cheese. According to folklore, the Virgin Mary lay on a bed of lady's bedstraw at the inn in Bethlehem, which led to the subsequent belief that a woman lying on a bed of the plant would have a safe childbirth.

This grassland was gloriously alluring in its sunny, protected aspect, and I lay down for a while soaking in the warmth as the gentle breeze ruffled the surrounding flowers and grasses. Meadow brown butterflies fluttered over the long grass in their droves and willow warblers sang from the trees that bordered its fringes.

The lepidopterist, Richard South, in his 1906 book, *The Butterflies of the British Isles*, maintained that the meadow brown's wide distribution and general abundance meant it could be regarded as the British Isles' commonest butterfly:

> It appears to be always on the wing in dull weather as well as in sunshine, and, except for a short interval in early August, it is to be seen in hayfields, open places in woods, or grassy slopes, or borders of highways and byways from June to September.

I'm not sure whether the meadow brown could be regarded as our commonest butterfly today, which is a direct reflection of the nationwide decline in meadows and grasslands, and where flowers are not so abundant in hayfields.

Another smaller butterfly floated past and landed briefly in the grass, before taking to the air and settling again. It was a large skipper, orange in hue, the wings folded back over the body, making it more akin to a moth than a butterfly. It was shy in demeanour, spiralling up into the air whenever I tried to approach. The skipper's eagerness to take flight upon my encroachment highlighted the excellent eyesight butterflies (and many other insects) have, being able to detect movement from a reasonable distance away. Skippers actively defend a patch of vegetation by driving away other skippers or flying insects that impinge upon their territory, and the skipper name comes from their habit of skipping from flower to flower and chasing away interlopers.

Large Skipper

Richard South described butterflies as 'aerial flowers', writing:

> The plants of woodland, meadow, moor or down have other 'blossoms' that arise from them, although they are not of them. These are the beautiful, winged creatures called butterflies, which as crawling caterpillars obtain their nourishment from plant leafage, and in the perfect state help the bees to rifle the flowers of their sweets, and at the same time assist in the work of fertilisation.

As I strolled through the grassland, his words held a special resonance, as the meadow browns and large skippers were indeed perfect, as were all the other insects and flowers in this little corner of Wales.

Chapter 15

SWEEPING MARSHES, MAJESTIC OAKS
& A BEREFT MALLARD

June 2022, Ceredigion

The River Teifi – or Afon Teifi as it is more properly known in Welsh – rises in the Cambrian Mountains in the county of Ceredigion and flows in a mainly southwesterly direction through beautiful undulating countryside before spilling out into the sea by the southern margin of Cardigan Bay. As it approaches the town of Cardigan, a pre-glacial channel left by the former course of the Teifi, and now occupied by the River Piliau, has created the Teifi Marshes, comprising a wonderful expanse of wetland with shimmering channels, open insect-buzzed pools and thick luscious reedbeds.

The Teifi Marshes send the mind slip-sliding away in eternal content-ment at the varied mosaic environment, which includes alder and willow carr, open pasture, woodland and tidal mudbanks. Managed by the Wildlife Trust of South & West Wales, the diversity in habitats over a relatively small area makes the marshes home to many different types of animals and plants, including dragonflies like the emperor, broad-bodied chaser, southern hawker and the scarce blue-tailed damselfly. In winter, the area is subject to extensive flooding and becomes a prolific sanctuary for waterfowl.

It was a gloriously sunny day, and after exploring some of the pools in an extensive area of reed bed, I followed a track through a broad wooded gorge by the edge of the Teifi. Fragments of slate littered the ground from historical quarrying and drifts of pink-tinged English stonecrop flowers gained fragile tenure by the quarry margins. For much of the nineteenth century, quarrying was a way of life here, comprising many small independent excavations as local farmers and estate owners took the opportunity to supplement their income by digging for slate. Whole communities were sustained by the slate industry and it remained a major employer in the area until the middle of the twentieth century. Today, the redundant quarries have been taken over by the soothing hand of nature and are home to lichens, bats and peregrine falcons, while hart's-tongue fern abound in the shadier recesses. This fern is so-called because the elongated shape of the leaves is said to resemble the tongue of a deer, with hart being an old term for a stag.

By the river's edge, a large splash from the water drew me to a nearby vantage point near which two large thick-lipped grey mullet languished just beneath the water surface. Grey mullet thrive in estuaries, where the slow-flowing water and rich muddy sediment provide ample algae and other food to satiate their appetites. The grey mullet is one of our most adaptable fishes and while they prefer estuaries, harbours and other sheltered areas of water, I have also encountered them when snorkelling in the clear, open seas of the northwest Highlands of Scotland. Their habit of swimming close to the surface makes them an easy target for ospreys and as these fish-eating raptors spread their range in England and Wales, mullet will most likely become a staple prey.

My return route led through a coppiced stretch of hazel woodland where dormice occur. It was a dark and enclosed place where the only sound came from a family party of great tits as they continually called to one another as they worked their way through the thick maze of hazel branches.

Keen to explore the Teifi and its surroundings further, I ventured a few kilometres upstream to the village of Cenarth, where a path followed the course of the river for a short distance, before looping along a quiet country lane back to the village. After a prolonged dry spell, the Teifi was running low, exposing a large rock shelf. In the middle of the shelf was a deep channel which the powerful erosive forces of the river had carved over the millennia. Swarms of mayflies danced over the channel and brown trout rippled the water as they rose to catch any insects that dared to linger upon the water surface.

A family of grey wagtails made the most of this mayfly bounty, the parent birds running busily backwards and forwards, and taking short intermittent flights to snap them out of the air. In one of the quieter pools, a mother mallard with a distinctive white pinion feather shepherded her single duckling while a wren churred from a nearby bramble tangle. Rising

Grey Wagtail

above the river swept a magnificent oak wood comprising mostly young trees. *This would be the perfect place for pied flycatchers,* I contemplated, especially once the woodland matured. Wales is renowned for its oak woodlands, which as well as pied flycatchers, is a favoured haunt for summer visiting redstarts and wood warblers, both of which are in decline nationally.

The importance of the oak to our environment is immense, a provider of life that creates abundant biodiversity through a domino effect of natural interdependence. The trunk and branches are characterised by numerous cracks and fissures, providing the perfect place for flora and fauna to gain a foothold and thrive. Oaks are long-lived, and an individual tree supports a multitude of different types of insects and other invertebrates, which themselves are fed upon by birds, bats, shrews and other creatures, not to mention the acorns that squirrels, jays and mice adore. Add the flora, fungi and other lifeforms, then the oak has the potential to support over 2,000 different species.

Over time, branches will be torn asunder from the trees in gales and the resultant holes and cracks create safe places for birds to nest. The fallen branches slowly decay on the woodland floor, providing another productive environment for a whole host of invertebrates and fungi to live. The leaves of oak rot easily, forming a rich leaf mould on the woodland floor. The oak is a pillar of life and a hallmark of British nature, which ensures it is a tree to be revered and cherished.

Such was the peaceful enchantment of this short river and woodland walk at Cenarth that I returned the following afternoon. I ventured out onto the rock shelf by the river once more where a small pool in a shallow depression on its hard surface brimmed with frog tadpoles. This was a precarious existence – should the river rise and turn to spate, the tadpoles would get washed away, and if the long dry spell continued, the pool would evaporate and they would surely succumb. It was a delicate balancing act of survival, entirely dependent on the vagaries of the weather.

Mother Mallard & Duckling

A short distance farther upstream, I caught sight of the same mother mallard with her distinctive white wing feather from the previous day, but she was alone this time and her single duckling had gone. Most likely she had hatched around eight youngsters only the previous week, all of which had perished. The river is an incredibly hazardous place for ducklings because of the ever-present threat from mink, otters, gulls, crows and buzzards.

Female mallards make excellent mothers, and this bereft duck brought the recollection of a fascinating encounter the previous year on my own local river, the Devon, in Scotland. There, I had stumbled upon a mother mallard with seven ducklings in tow. On detecting my presence, she uttered a soft call to alert the ducklings of imminent danger. Immediately, all seven of her wee fluffy bundles gathered, and purposefully, but with great care to ensure there was no tell-tale ripple from their water wakes, sidled into the far bank and crammed themselves under alder roots.

There was no room for the mother in this bankside recess, so instead she lay frozen and prostrate nearby upon the water's edge – half her body on the muddy bank and her head pointing downwards into the river with her bill partially submerged, so that she could just breathe. In effect, she was imitating a small log that was half-in and half-out of the water, the body outline totally broken-up by merging herself between river and land. It was a remarkable piece of camouflage, a flamboyant exhibition of guile to protect her precious ducklings. After all, this was her raison d'être; to keep the mallard generations going, or to be more precise, to pass on her own genetic lineage.

This leads to the obvious questions. *How did she know to do that, to duck and to dive, if you pardon the pun, to instinctively use such trickery to conceal herself and her brood from potential threat? Had she seen her own mother react in the same way when she herself was a duckling and learnt from that – or is such behaviour genetic and pre-programmed?* I suspect it is all wired into the genes, although this is probably aided by learning from experience to fine-tune such tactics.

Alas, this female on the Teifi had lost in the lottery of nature, but there was every chance she would survive until next spring, when with that bit of extra experience, the odds were stacked more in her favour of rearing one or more ducklings to the holy grail of adulthood.

_____

Chapter 16

A SURPRISE DOLPHIN ENCOUNTER
& ENDANGERED ANGELSHARKS

June 2022, Ceredigion

On the coast of the southern part of Cardigan Bay nestles the charming town of New Quay, with its small harbour and attractive houses that cling tenaciously to a steep slope that rises above the sea.

New Quay was a chance visit as my intention was to head farther north towards Aberystwyth but on seeing the signpost on the road, I instinctively took the turning out of curiosity. As a stranger to the area, I had never heard of New Quay before, but on ambling down a narrow lane towards the harbour, the throngs of visitors highlighted that this was a popular holiday destination.

The attraction was obvious, for it was a picturesque location, although there was a twinge of disappointment as it did not seem a likely haven for wildlife. Nonetheless, I continued down to the harbour and sat on the breakwater wall, which provided the perfect spot to have a bite to eat and plan where next to visit.

As I munched on a sandwich, a herring gull, which was perched on the gunwale of a nearby moored boat, took to the air in a flurry of wings and swooped down upon a piece of bread that had been tossed into the water by a child. The herring gull is the perennial opportunist and is equally content following a trawler at sea, turning over the surface of a rubbish tip or scavenging the contents of discarded fast-food containers in city centres on a Saturday night.

Despite this close association with humankind, herring gulls are declining in Britain, perhaps because there are fewer opportunities for them to scavenge, including from fishing industry discards. The herring gull is now in the 'red' category as a bird of serious conservation concern such has been the fall in breeding numbers, which in recent times has been further fuelled by Avian Influenza (Bird Flu). Nonetheless, the population is still higher than it was at the start of the twentieth century and perhaps numbers are adjusting to a new equilibrium. Herring gulls are loathed by many people, but they are clever birds and deserve our respect.

I finished the sandwich, rose to my feet, and looked over the harbour wall out to sea. In a jaw-dropping moment of surprise, the fin of a bottlenose dolphin broke the surface only about 200 m away, and two more dolphins appeared slightly farther offshore. On my way down to the harbour, I had seen adverts for boat trips out in the bay to see dolphins but it never occurred to me that they might venture so close to the harbour. I managed to reel-off a few photographs before the dolphins disappeared as quickly as they had materialised. It was a breathtaking encounter and totally unexpected, leaving every fibre in my body tingling with exhilaration.

Bottlenose Dolphin

Cardigan Bay is home to one of only two semi-resident groups of bottlenose dolphins in Britain; the other is in the Moray Firth in Scotland. The Welsh population is slightly larger than the Scottish one, with there being up to 250 animals present, although not all at the same time. There is evidence that in recent years some of the Cardigan Bay dolphin population are regularly moving farther afield and spending some of their time off other parts of the Welsh coast or beyond.

If this is the case, it interestingly coincides with a recent change in behaviour in the Moray Firth dolphins, where some animals frequently venture down the east coast as far south as Yorkshire. It is not fully understood why the Moray Firth dolphins are doing this, but it is likely related to a steady increase in total population size (with associated evidence of increased survival rates and reproductive rates) and the distribution of sources of prey. Previous research has shown that areas of high use for bottlenose dolphins in Scotland are also important foraging areas, and it is likely there are similar areas off the northeast English coastline that have a relatively high prey abundance.

Bottlenose dolphins are one reason Cardigan Bay is designated as a Special Area of Conservation, as indeed is much of the Welsh coast. The bay is rich in marine life with sunfish, basking sharks and leatherback turtles occasional summer visitors, while seabirds gather in large numbers during the breeding season. The bay features shallow reefs and sandbanks that are home to a variety of fish, seaweeds and invertebrates, making it an Aladdin's Cave of natural wealth. The westerly aspect of the vast bay collects the prevailing winds and waves, and combined with the shallow depth of the water, acts like a giant mixing cauldron, swirling up nutrients from the seabed to the benefit of wildlife.

The critically-endangered angelshark occurs in Cardigan Bay and it is thought they may even breed in Welsh waters. It is a mysterious bottom-dwelling fish, with grey skin and a flattened body that can grow up to almost 2 m in length. They have been recorded off Wales since the early nineteenth century and several different names are accorded to the species including monkfish, banjofish and jakie shark. Another name is puppyfish, perhaps because rather than laying eggs, it is viviparous, giving birth to up to 25 pups in one go, which are perfect miniatures of their parents. The tough skin of the angelshark was once used by the Romans to cover shields and sword handles. Angelsharks prey upon flatfish, gobies and crustaceans and are occasionally found in very shallow water. In 2020, the Wales Angelshark Action Plan was launched to encourage priority conservation actions and to address research gaps.

Intrigued by the marine life of the area, I ventured a couple of kilometres farther north to Little Quay, or Cei Bach as it is known. This sand and shingle beach was delightfully quiet compared to the hustle and bustle of New Quay, and with the tide out, I guddled around in a handful of pools at one end of the beach in search of sea creatures. The sun shone down warm, the sea was mirror-calm and it was wonderfully relaxing turning over rocks and stones to see what natural treasures were revealed beneath. Small fish proved elusive, but on turning one rock, a tiny cuttlefish scooted out, no more than a few centimetres long. It stopped for a second, then quickly buried itself in the sand so that I was unable to find it again. Cuttlefish are fascinating cephalopods, which are related to the squid and octopus. A few years previously, I encountered several adult cuttlefish when snorkelling near Mojácar in Spain, their tiger-striped bodies gliding just over the seabed like mini-hovercraft. These cuttlefish were always shy, rocketing away in a sudden burst of speed whenever I approached too close.

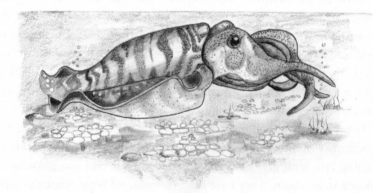

Cuttlefish

I turned over more rocks in the hope of revealing other cuttlefish, but to no avail. Instead, my attention turned to a cluster of periwinkles. Like the herring gull I had witnessed at New Quay, for most people, periwinkles barely merit a second glance because of their familiarity, but when seen up close they are shining jewels, with intricate spiralled patterns on their shells. There are several periwinkle species in British waters, the most colourful is the flat periwinkle, which is often bright yellow or orange.

In my late teens, I camped for a few days on a remote section of the Berwickshire coast to try and live a self-sufficient existence from the fruits of the land and sea in an experimental challenge of survival skills. I had no luck catching fish with my rod and line and instead resorted to winkles as my main source of food, which I boiled in a tin can on a primus stove and used a fishing hook to scoop out the meat. They tasted salty and while palatable, I soon tired of their monotony, leaving my self-sufficiency exercise one of ignominy due to its hastened abandonment. While winkles may be an acquired taste, commercial winkle harvesting is still big business in Britain and the shellfish are in good demand in France and other parts of Europe. They were an important food in Britain in earlier times and in nineteenth century London it is estimated that three million pints of winkles were sold each year as street food.

On turning over another rock, a small brown shrimp scuttled out. As with my previous encounter with the baby cuttlefish, it quickly disappeared into the sand. Like the winkle, brown shrimps were once hugely popular in parts of Britain as food, often mixed with butter and sealed in jars as potted shrimps. They are still in strong demand and there are active fisheries today in Morecambe Bay and some other parts of Britain.

Finding the cluster of winkles and glimpsing the shrimp was a reminder of the importance of our seas as a source of food. In contrast, the earlier dolphin encounter and the knowledge that angelsharks lived in the waters of Cardigan Bay was an awakening call of the need to conserve our precious marine life. As well as food, the world depends upon healthy seas for numerous reasons, not least as a controller of climate. All life, whether terrestrial or aquatic depends upon clean and vibrant seas for their existence. Oceans are the beating heart of the planet and even have the potential to form part of future global energy supply solutions.

Fish and shellfish are an essential part of global food security and important for a healthy diet. The challenge is to manage our seas in a way that does not impinge upon fishing livelihoods and food supply, yet which at the same time offers effective protection to the marine environment. If we get that right, our oceans have the potential to be a sustainable provider of low carbon footprint food far into the future, whilst providing an eternal source of wonder at the beauty and diversity of life held within.

When turning over one final rock, I held my breath in anticipation at what other miracle of nature might materialise beneath, such was the wealth of wild riches that prospered in this vast Welsh bay. A tiny fish scooted out, so fast it was a mere blur in the shallows, and quickly sought refuge under another rock. I began to turn over that rock too, but on reflection gently eased it back into place. Much better, I thought, to leave this small fish in peace and let its identity remain a tantalising mystery.

Chapter 17

HARDY DAISIES & ELEGANT KITES

June 2022, Powys

After several days of hot weather in Pembrokeshire, Carmarthenshire and Ceredigion, it was a relief to feel the cool breeze and the misty rain against my face in this remote part of the Cambrian Mountains between Ponterwyd and Llangurig in Powys. The sea was some distance away and it was inspiring to be in the heart of Wales, a landscape of rounded hills, gushing streams and patchwork woodland. The surrounding mountains and hills, with their numerous folds and spurs, hold a plethora of wildlife secrets that cry out for exploration. Many of the hills are a good height, including Pen Pumlumon Fawr, which rises to over 700 m. My intention had been to climb to the top of one, but I soon abandoned the idea because of the low cloud and swirling mist and adopted instead to explore a nearby forestry plantation.

The track running through the forest was wide and the margins sparkled with upland flowers such as heath bedstraw and bilberry (blaeberry). There were also daisies, but their flowers were closed because of the light drizzle. Daises are to be admired because these beautiful little flowers are the epitome of resilience, prospering throughout much of Britain, including in impoverished upland habitats. On our garden lawns they are brutally trimmed weekly, yet always bounce back in their white-flowered brilliance. The daisy is remarkable in that there is barely a month in the year when there are not at least some daisies out in flower, even in darkest winter. John Clare in his journal for 1824 noted that he 'gatherd a handful of daiseys in full bloom on Christmas Day'.

The daisy was Chaucer's favourite flower thanks to its cheery demeanour which he wrote 'could soften my sorrow'. The name daisy is a derivation of 'day's eye', a reflection of the yellow orb revealed when the delicate white petals open in the morning and which resembles the sun. And, of course, daisies are an irresistible pull for insects, attracting a range of pollinators and making a typical lawn a thriving place for wildlife.

Other flowers that shone out from this forest track included herb-bennet (wood aven) and a last-breath cuckooflower, hanging on in bloom much later than normal. Rowan flowers were similarly coming to an end, their former snowy-white magnificence now grey and impoverished. In only a few weeks' time, however, this lost lament to spring would turn into a glorious herald of autumn as the rowan's scarlet berries begin to develop.

This plant life got me thinking about commercial conifer plantations. The conventional wisdom among many environmentalists is that they are bad for biodiversity, but this is a view I have never fully subscribed to. True, the ground beneath a thick blanket of towering spruces is bare and largely devoid of life, but plantations are typically criss-crossed with access tracks that act like sunny glades, bursting with wildflowers and insects. Once a plantation matures and felling commences, a varied habitat is produced of rotating sun-kissed open areas and new plantings. Certainly, many parts of a mature conifer plantation are more biodiverse than heavily-grazed adjacent areas of open hill, and fast-growing plantations can play an important role in carbon capture.

A red kite briefly appeared over a gap in the trees, its forked tail twisting in the breeze as it maintained its determined course. It seemed entirely appropriate to have glimpsed this kite because not so long ago the British population was confined to the hills of central Wales where only a handful of breeding pairs grimly hung on for survival.

Richard Fitter, the prolific bird guidebook writer, wrote in the 1970 edition of the *Collins Guide to Birdwatching*:

> Those who wish to make the acquaintance of the kite in Wales are urged not to try to do so during the nesting season, from April to July, for our dozen or so pairs of breeding kites are very shy birds and have been known to desert their nests merely because of some picnickers nearby. Moreover, they are still threatened by egg collectors, and swarms of rubber-necking birdwatchers make the tasks of wardening the nests much harder.

The kite's change of fortune has been remarkable following a series of reintroduction schemes throughout Britain, which first began in 1989 in the Chilterns and near Inverness on the Black Isle. The spur was the realisation that the slow rate of population expansion in Wales meant that there was little chance of kites spreading their wings any time soon to other parts of Britain. The reintroductions, initially using birds from Germany and Sweden, have been so successful that there are now approaching 2,000 breeding pairs in Britain, with about half in Wales and the rest in England and Scotland. They have also been reintroduced to Northern Ireland.

Red Kite

It was just the kick-start the kites needed, the habitat was there and, as importantly, the transformation in human perception was there, with a relaxation in formerly negative attitudes about birds of prey by landowners, which of course, was bolstered by bird protection legislation.

Several more kites soared above me and a buzzard mewed in the distance, another bird of prey that has dramatically increased its range in recent decades, albeit in this case under its own steam. On a lone sycamore that stood apart in a forest clearing, a family of coal tits busied themselves, calling all the time to keep in contact with one another as the parents feverishly scoured the maple-shaped leaves for caterpillars.

Coal tits are one of the few songbirds that thrive in coniferous plantations. Their small size and great agility enable them to glean tiny invertebrate food from inbetween pine needles with their thin bills. In a fascinating evolutionary twist, Continental coal tits have even narrower bills than their British counterparts because they specialise in conifer woodlands to a much greater extent. In Ireland, where there are fewer conifers, coal tits have larger bills than their British cousins. It is evolutionary adaptation on a par with the finches of the Galapagos Islands in the Pacific, which were the founding basis of Charles Darwin's ground-breaking book, *On the Origin of Species.*

Coal Tit

Coal tits also feed on conifer seeds and in winters when the seed crop is poor, they are far more likely to venture into our gardens. Watching the interaction between coal tits, and the larger blue and great tits on a garden bird table is always fascinating. The great tit will take no nonsense from other birds and will spread its wings and hiss to protect its own little bit of space on the hanging peanut or seed dispenser. Indeed, when I used to put leg rings on birds for study purposes, the great tit was always the species most likely to give a nasty nip from its sharp beak.

Blue tits similarly show a degree of aggression should an interloper get in the way. The smaller coal tit, on the other hand, just gets on with things. Coal tits adore sunflower seeds; a pair can empty a seed dispenser in no time at all. They zip backwards and forwards like busy little bees, but they are only eating some of the sunflower seeds, the rest are hidden away in nooks and crannies in the garden to be consumed later. They are intriguing little birds and storing food is a useful survival strategy.

For the family of coal tits foraging in this solitary sycamore in the Cambrian Mountains, the broad leaves of the sycamore must have seemed like an oasis rich in food compared with the harder pickings to be had from the nearby spruces. Nonetheless, they soon exhausted the sycamore of its rich bounty, and in an undulating flight, darted away back into the depths of the forest, their thin wispy calls fading under a grey-shrouded sky.

_____

Chapter 18

PARCHED EARTH & THE MIRACLE OF
OSPREY MIGRATION

August 2022, Leicestershire & Rutland

The ravages of the long, hot summer were stark to the eye in this little Leicestershire meadow, which overlooked the Vale of Belvoir and the Trent Valley. The once verdant green carpet that would have shimmered here only a few weeks previously had transformed into a field of parched straw, where no wildflowers bloomed and few insects buzzed.

Coombs Meadows, which nestles on a slope above the village of Stathern, is a nature reserve belonging to the Leicestershire & Rutland Wildlife Trust, and is a grassland where ragged robin, greater bird's-foot trefoil and the locally scarce whorl grass occur. In spring, marsh marigolds bloom, as does betony later in the summer. Meadow saxifrage and common spotted orchids are also found here.

While this was early August and most of the spring and early summer plants had naturally finished flowering, the parched soil and desiccated vegetation was not how things should have been and was a telling reminder of the impact of climate change on our precious landscape. It was a depressing scene that sent me numb with shock. Coombs Meadow looked more reminiscent of the Mediterranean region in late summer rather than a vista from England's green and pleasant land.

It was a similar story at Cossington Meadows, a former gravel works on the northern outskirts of Leicester by the River Soar. Ditches and pools were dried up and bereft of life. By a diminishing puddle of water, which was the remnants of a large pond, a lone black-headed gull sat forlornly. The sun beamed down in excruciating fashion and nature was silent under the baking heat. Wading birds such as redshanks, lapwings and little ringed plovers nest by the pools at Cossington Meadows and one wondered how their chicks would be able to cope with the receding fresh water where damp muddy margins, formerly rich in invertebrate life, were now hard baked like concrete. Grass snakes, too, would be suffering, and I pondered whether their only means of survival would be to seek out the last remnants of mud and water, and rest in torpor in the thick ooze until the life-enhancing rains replenished the pools and ditches once more.

And, of course, there was the plight faced by fish and the amphibians – the more one thought about the impact of this drought, the more heartbreaking became the realisation of the havoc being wrought. Blackbirds and song thrushes would find the hard ground unyielding and impossible to forage upon for worms and other invertebrates. In nearby woodlands, worm-loving badgers would be suffering similar hardship, while trees endured stress and plants in the surrounding countryside withered. This was an unmitigated disaster for wildlife.

It is not just the land that is impacted by such searing heat. Data published by the Centre for Environment, Fisheries and Aquaculture Science reveals that sea temperatures across the south and east of England hit record-breaking levels during the summer of 2022. In the southern North Sea, water temperatures were above 20 degrees Celsius for several weeks. Across the rest of Britain, temperatures at Liverpool Bay, the Moray Firth, the Hebrides and the Firth of Forth all reached above average levels. Research shows that warmer seas are already having an impact on the move-ment and behaviour of fish stocks throughout the seas off the British Isles.

The bushes by the trackside at Cossington Meadows comprised a mix of species, including elder and blackthorn, both of which held fruits. The elderberries hung in dark, grape-like bunches, whilst the vinous sloes clung in small clusters to the prickly branches of the blackthorns. I plucked a sloe and bit tentatively into it – the flavour was sour and acrid. Sloes are certainly an acquired taste. I am very much taken by this verdict on the dubiety of their flavour written by William Cobbett in 1825:

> This pulp, which I have eaten many times as a boy
> until my tongue clove to the roof of my mouth and my
> lips were pretty much glued together, is astringent
> beyond the powers of alum.

Elderberries are similarly bitter and tart when eaten raw, and because they are mildly poisonous, should be cooked first to remove the toxins. Elderberries make excellent wine and jam, and are naturally rich in Vitamin C. Whether elder is a tree or a shrub is a topic for debate, but whatever the case, one of my earliest nature memories from childhood was the distinctive, unpleasant smell that emanated from their leaves. The malodourous aroma was said to have once been used by drovers to deter flies from their cattle, although I am unconvinced whether elder is a proven insect deterrent. What is indisputable is that the elder was much revered for its medicinal qualities. A cordial made from elder was used to treat colds, coughs and bronchitis, and the leaves were believed to help bruises and strains. The medieval herbalist John Evelyn wrote:

> If the medicinal properties of its leaves, bark and berries were fully known, I cannot tell what our countryman could ail for which he might not fetch a remedy from every hedge, either for sickness, or wounds.

While the Coombs and Cossington meadow lands were arid and unforgiving, water was mercifully still in plentiful supply at Rutland Water farther to the east, where it was uplifting to watch a whole host of water birds on the mirror-calm surface. Built in the 1970s, Rutland Water is the largest man-made lake by surface area in England at 1,555 hectares. The reservoir has a large nature reserve area (182 hectares) on its western side, which holds several important designations including a Site of Special Scientific Interest and a European Special Protection Area and is considered an internationally important wetland site. Managed by the Leicestershire & Rutland Wildlife Trust in partnership with Anglian Water, it provides one of the most important wildfowl sanctuaries in Britain.

There are two main points of entry for the nature reserve. I opted for the one at the Lyndon Visitor Centre, from where I wandered along a path adjacent to the southern shore edge. Large rafts of moulting great crested grebes and mute swans drifted out on the water; on the banksides lapwings and mallards rested, dowdy and unkempt as they too moulted. Summer's end was approaching, and the wildfowl were shedding their old feathers and reinvigorating themselves with the new.

In one of the shallow shore pools by an observation hide, a little egret carefully trod the margins in search of fish and frogs. Farther away, over a drift of reeds, a great white egret momentarily appeared in a slow and lazy flight before it descended into the reedbed and became lost from view. The skeletal branches of a long dead tree held several cormorants, their dark bodies contrasting starkly with the brilliance of the azure sky backdrop.

I ventured to another hide which overlooked Manton Bay, where an adult and two young ospreys lazed, one on a pole sticking out the water, the other two perched on a half-submerged tree trunk. The young had fledged the nearby nest, which was built on the top of an artificial platform especially erected to encourage them to breed. As with red kites, the breeding ospreys at Rutland Water are the result of an innovative translocation project, which began in 1996 when osprey chicks from Scottish nests were released. In 2001, the first pair began breeding and today over 200 ospreys have fledged from nests in the Rutland Water area. The breeding population is now self-sustaining and the Rutland ospreys are spreading their wings to colonise other parts of England and Wales, and even the Netherlands.

Ospreys Over Rutland Water

The crucial difference between the Rutland Water osprey introduction compared with red kites and white-tailed eagles in Britain is that ospreys are migratory, spending the winter mostly in west Africa, especially Senegal and Gambia. This was a challenge that conservationists overcame, with young Scottish osprey chicks translocated at six weeks old into special holding pens overlooking Rutland Water, which gave the birds a wide-ranging view over the reservoir. The young were fed trout pushed through small hatches into the pens to avoid disturbance and minimise contact with people.

Once released, the young ospreys soon habituated themselves to their new watery environment, honing their inbuilt fishing skills and living the dream of being free and wild. Then, they embarked upon their solo migrations – all young ospreys do this, there are no parents to follow, instead they rely upon pre-wired instructions in the brain.

Ospreys migrate alone, and a juvenile's first migration is a monumental challenge. Around 70 per cent of ospreys perish in their first few years, often ending by dropping exhausted into the sea because of navigational errors. Over time, however, those that survive learn the best routes and fishing and resting spots during migration, and can lead long lives, rearing many chicks in the process.

My return route from the Rutland Water osprey hide took me past a vibrant hedge where blue and red damselflies danced, and gatekeeper butterflies flitted on flashing wings. Gatekeeper is a most appropriate name as this enchanting butterfly is often

Gatekeeper Butterfly

encountered where clumps of flowers grow by gateways and along hedgerows, where it is also sometimes known as the hedge brown. It is one of the last butterflies to emerge in summer and is an attractive insect, with orange-brown burnished wings. Common in much of England and Wales, the species is expanding its range northwards – another indication of our warming climate and the way our nature is changing at unparalleled pace.

Chapter 19

BIZARRE SPOONBILLS & NATURE
ON THE MOVE

August 2022, Lincolnshire

A group of large, white heron-like birds huddled together on an islet in a freshwater pool by the huge shallow sea bay of The Wash, one of Britain's most important havens for wildlife. They were spoonbills and I was thrilled to see such a large gathering of these scarce British birds.

I was at the RSPB reserve of Frampton Marsh, near Boston in Lincoln-shire, which was experiencing a bumper year for spoonbills, with over 50 birds having been spotted on at least one occasion. The group I was watching was smaller at around 20 birds, and all were quietly slumbering with their long bills tucked underwing. Occasionally, a head would pop out from beneath a wing to reveal a long bill with spoon-shaped tip, which would then be quickly hidden again under the snuggled embrace of the feathers.

Spoonbills, Frampton Marsh

The remarkable spatulate bill of the spoonbill is a design that borders on the bizarre. It is used to good effect in shallow water to glean tiny invertebrates and small fish in a rhythmic sideways, sweeping motion. In times past, in this part of England, the bird was known as the 'shovlerere' or 'shovelard', but I think shovel is too grand a term when referring to the bill, and spoon is far more appropriate, for it is an intricate instrument of precision.

I hesitate to mention global warming again, but its impact was becoming increasingly apparent during my British wildlife exploration, and the expansion in the range of spoonbills into Britain is no doubt aided in part by climate change, possibly because more typical haunts in the Mediterranean are drying up. Great white egrets, cattle egrets and black-winged stilts have all established colonies in Britain in recent years. However, the spoonbill's recovery, and indeed that of other water birds is as much related to conservation work in restoring suitable wetlands, which have seen an expansion in their range in northern Europe, most notably in the Netherlands where many of the English colonisers hail from.

Furthermore, spoonbills are native to Britain, have been recorded since Anglo Saxon times and are an integral part of the island's fauna. Spoonbills disappeared from their last British stronghold in East Anglia by the middle of the seventeenth century due to the drainage of wetlands and by hunting for food. They have slowly increased in numbers over the last few decades and are now established breeders at places such as Holkham National Nature Reserve in Norfolk.

Near where the spoonbills rested at Frampton Marsh, several avocets fed quietly by the bank margins. Avocets too have unusual long bills, which are curved upwards in a shallow U-shape. They are elegant waders with their stunning black and white plumage and delicate build. Like the spoonbill, avocets were formerly lost as breeding birds in Britain by the middle of the nineteenth century, before they began to recolonise again just after the Second World War on Havergate Island in Suffolk. They have since spread and now breed in various parts of southern and central England, and the bird is perhaps best known as the logo of the RSPB.

As I watched an avocet feed in a shallow ditch, one could instantly see that the upturned bill was a perfect adaptation for sifting small creatures from the water, as a long straight beak would not provide the same

Avocet

coverage across the surface when being swept from side to side. Avocets wade deeply and sometimes swim and up-end like a dabbling duck. In Lincolnshire, an old name for the avocet is 'yelper' in reference to their alarm call, especially when their chicks come under threat.

Frampton Marsh was a lively place for birds, not least because the pre-autumn migration season was underway. In a pool nearby, a curlew sandpiper waded by the edge. The curlew sandpiper is a small wader, slightly larger than the much more common dunlin to which it is super-ficially similar. Curlew sandpipers breed on the Arctic tundra of Siberia and winter in Africa, and this one still sported the remnants of its summer chestnut breeding plumage. The east coast of Britain is a stopping-over point for curlew sandpipers when on migration, the sandpipers attracted by estuaries and coastal pools and scrapes in places such as Frampton Marsh. Herein lay another reminder that nature conservation must be co-ordin-ated on an international basis because if there were no stopover refuelling points for curlew sandpipers, their population would rapidly dwindle.

Nearby, another larger migratory wader, a ruff, probed the mud with its stout, slightly downturned bill. This ruff looked unremarkable in appearance, largely beige with mottled feathers. I couldn't tell whether it was a male or a female, but if the former, then only a couple of months previously it would have been adorned with a colourful ruff around the head and neck, which it would have used for displaying to court females. The colour of the ruff varies among individuals, ranging from orange to cream to buff, and many tints and hues inbetween. The courtship occurs on specially selected areas of ground known as leks, which are display arenas where females gather to watch the males dance and perform by bowing their heads and flaring their ruffs. Behind the dull cloak of this plain-looking wading bird at Frampton Marsh lay a real dandy of a performer and a creature of mystique.

The pools at Frampton were fascinating to explore and flourished with black-tailed godwits, teal, redshanks and greylag geese. A lone barnacle goose lingered in one watery corner, but rather than an arrival from traditional Arctic breeding grounds, this one was most likely an escapee from a private bird collection. It was an unusually hot day and common blue butterflies danced by the path edges, as well as a lone painted lady.

Painted lady butterflies are forever a source of wonderment because they are long-distance migrants from North Africa. While it was entirely possible this one had migrated here all the way from Africa in one go, much more likely it was the progeny of a butterfly that had headed north from African shores in spring and then bred in Continental Europe, from where the newly emerged butterfly continued northwards as if a participant in a relay race. The urge to migrate north is probably triggered when painted lady densities in a particular area become so great that their caterpillars start to strip bare food plants and can no longer survive, thus they move on to find pastures new. In some years, painted ladies are abundant in Britain, in others scarce.

I headed up to a grassy sea wall, and from its brow the vast expanse of The Wash lay beyond, yet with the tide out and the shimmering heat haze, it was impossible to discern the sea with any clarity. The Wash is a huge bay fringed by wetlands, saltmarshes and tidal rivers where expansive mudflats are exposed when the tide recedes. It is one of Britain's most important winter-feeding areas for waders and wildfowl, and where grey and harbour seals have traditional pupping sites.

I sat on the grassy bank and breathed in the warm air, revelling in the wide, open horizons. A hobby swept over a distant bed of reeds, its flight erratic as it hunted for dragonflies. A small flock of black-tailed godwits wheeled overhead before tumbling down to one of the pools in the marsh. The vastness of the landscape was overwhelming, which made me feel very small. Yet, in a strange and inexplicable way this feeling of insignificance made me feel part of the environment, in tune with its buzz of life and where I could sense every change and nuance, and it was incredibly uplifting.

Chapter 20

A PLASTIC ABOMINATION
& A TIDAL RAINFOREST

October 2022, Yorkshire

As the shingle crunched under my footfall on the seaward side of Spurn Point, gleaming white shards caught the autumnal sun, glinting and dancing like a random scattering of quartz crystals. Unfortunately, this was not a natural sprinkling of dazzling mineral deposits but was instead plastic, or to be more precise, the remnants of white plastic cups.

Plastic Cup, Shingle Beach

I may be wrong and it is only a guess, but it seems plausible that the abundance of the same type of plastic cup on this beach was the result of passengers throwing them overboard from the ferries that ply daily between Hull and the Continent. If so, this was a quick fix pleasure with horrendous long-term consequences – down a coffee or tea in ten minutes and toss the cup over the side of the ship, only for the plastic to pollute the environment for hundreds of years to come.

It was a sorry scene and one I had become all too familiar with in recent years, from my local river in Scotland to the storm-tossed shores of Skye, and even wild and remote beaches in Costa Rica – *plastic, plastic everywhere and not a jot do people think*. Once plastic is in the ocean, it decomposes very slowly, breaking into tiny microplastics, which can enter the marine food chain and become hugely damaging to sea life. It is estimated that at least 14 million tons of plastic end up in the ocean every year, and plastic makes up to 80 per cent of all marine debris found from surface waters to deep-sea sediments. As well as the impact on wildlife, plastic pollution threatens food safety and quality, human health, coastal tourism and contributes to climate change.

The plastic cups on this beach at the mouth of the Humber estuary was intensely depressing and a reminder of how we all need to change our reliance on plastics. Of course, plastic is a wonderful invention and material, with so many uses from construction to packaging – but we need to find alternatives where possible, and we need to recycle more. This is a challenge for government, businesses and of course individuals. It is madness, for example, for a hotel to stock disposable plastic cups in guest rooms, when using long-life plastic cups (or glass) as an alternative would dramatically reduce waste and benefit the environment. Consumer power is key, and if the pressure is there, then businesses, whether in the manufacturing or service sectors, will quickly adapt and respond.

I turned my mind away from plastic and to the peninsula at Spurn Point, which curves out as a narrow spit, bounded by the North Sea on one side and the Humber estuary on the other. The spit is over 5 km long and just 45 m wide in places. This was an environment of two halves: the seaward side splashed with rolling, white crested wave tops, while the sheltered estuary was calm and benign. From my vantage point on the low brow, I could see both with barely a turn of the head.

A short while before, near the Yorkshire Wildlife Trust's Spurn National Nature Reserve visitor centre, I had watched a young black-tailed godwit paddle in a reedy, saltmarsh pool. From there, I headed out towards the point, passing orange-berried sea buckthorn bushes, one of which held a small flock of restless reed buntings. The leaves of sea buckthorn are willow-like, and it is a pioneer species, able to colonise nutrient-poor areas of ground such as shingle coasts, having the ability to take nitrogen from the air and 'fix' it in the ground in a way that boosts soil fertility. It is a widespread coastal shrub of eastern Britain, although never common. Its berries are avidly sought out by fieldfares, redwings and migrant blackbirds in autumn when they make landfall after having crossed the North Sea.

Black-tailed Godwit

The exposed easterly location of Spurn Point makes it attractive for migrants, and the day before my visit, scarce eastern European songbirds such as yellow-browed warbler and barred warbler had been recorded. I did not spot any such rarities, but there was a definite movement of commoner migrants passing over, especially meadow pipits, as well as a lone ring ouzel, which is similar in shape and form to a blackbird, and which nests in mountain areas.

Spurn is a dynamic strip of fragile land that never stands still, constantly changing and moving in a westerly direction. It was formed by the phenomenon known as longshore drift, where sediment eroded by the sea is washed along the coast, and at the mixing point where the North Sea meets the Humber, the sediment builds up to form a peninsula made from sand and shingle.

An extremely high tidal surge in 2013 washed away a section of road and sand dune, resulting in Spurn becoming a temporary tidal island whenever high spring tides flowed across the middle section of the peninsula, cutting it off from the mainland. Since then, the part of the spit in this vulnerable wash-over area has moved significantly towards the estuary and in the process built up over 2 m of sand dune, providing new protection, resulting in tidal surges being less able to breach the peninsula.

About halfway out towards the point lay a designated seagrass protection area, where seagrass seeds have been planted by conservationists on
the estuarine tidal mudflats to extend the area of existing meadow.
Research shows that the UK has lost at least 44 per cent of its seagrass since
1936. Seagrass meadows have the ability to capture and store more carbon
than an equivalent area of tropical rainforest and form a valuable habitat
for a host of marine creatures. Seagrass, or eelgrass, is not a seaweed but
instead a flowering plant that lives on the lower shore down to about 10 m
in depth. Their meadows are home to creatures such as pipefish, a relative
of the seahorse, and form nursery grounds for commercial fish species like
plaice. The meadows typically grow in sheltered areas like estuaries and
bays and are an important food source for grazing geese and wigeon, whilst
the roots stabilise the sediment, helping prevent erosion on the seabed.

This tidal rainforest on the Humber is a crucial ecosystem worthy of
protection and the new plantings will help it prosper in the years to come.
I scrutinised a distant dark green patch of seagrass through my binoculars,
and as I swung the eyepieces round in a broad half-arc, I picked out shelduck,
curlews, redshanks and grey and ringed plovers foraging in the mud.

I turned full circle and brought the binoculars to bear over the North
Sea, where muddy-brown rollers broke against the beach in a wild and
crazy surge. Close inshore, a grey seal porpoised through the water,
continually half breaching in a rolling motion. I do not know why the seal
was doing this, but I speculated it might have been doing so for fun. After
all, sadness and joy are not just emotions confined to humanity, which is
something we should never forget, especially when ensuring high animal
welfare standards in agriculture.

On my return to the Spurn visitor centre, I scoured the buckthorn one
last time for migrant songbirds. Whilst there was no detectable movement
other than a lone robin, I suspected that deep within the prickly buckthorn
cover, windblown migrants would be sheltering, exhausted from their
hazardous North Sea crossing and were waiting until nightfall, before
slipping away under the cover of darkness to embark upon the next stage
of their marathon journeys.

Chapter 21

MERMAID'S PURSES, 'RICE KRISPIES' WHELK EGGS & A PRICKLY DUNE DWELLER

October 2022, Flintshire

A blustery wind whipped across beach and mudflats at the mouth of the wild and empty Dee Estuary in northeast Wales, and as is my habit in such places, my eyes were continually drawn to the sand as I sought out mollusc half-shells and other natural debris from the sea.

The sea air was invigorating, an empowering elixir that freshened the mind and heightened the senses. A dark, leathery pouch on the sand caught my attention – the egg capsule of a ray, colloquially known as a 'mermaid's purse'. I gently picked it up and cradled this miracle from the sea in the palm of my hand, making sure the strong wind didn't whisk it away. The capsule was rectangular in shape, with four horn-like tendrils on each corner. It was most probably the egg case of a thornback ray, but I was not sure of my identification as those of blonde rays and spotted rays are similar in form.

A female thornback ray typically lays less than a hundred eggs each year on shallow sand, mud, pebble or gravel bottoms. This is a very low reproductive rate, especially when one considers that a single cod can lay millions of eggs at one time. As such, ray populations are inherently vulnerable. They are fascinating fish, with their powerful jaws on the underside of the body perfectly designed for feeding upon hard-bodied creatures such as shrimps and crabs.

While thornbacks are usually found in depths of 2-60 m, they can occur down to 600 m, and have an annual cycle of migration from deeper offshore waters during autumn and winter, migrating to inshore waters in spring to breed. Rays are perhaps more widely regarded as inhabitants of warmer, tropical seas, but at least a dozen different species occur in British waters, including electric rays and stingrays.

The beach here close to the village of Talacre in Flintshire is a popular spot for day-trippers and holidaymakers in the summer and at weekends, but on this blustery autumnal morning it was desolate and empty. Buoyed by the mermaid's purse, my eyes continued to scan the beach and other interesting finds were soon unveiled, including a cluster of whelk eggs, which looked like a congealed mass of Rice Krispies breakfast cereal.

The half-shells of razorshells were scattered widely on the beach and in some places had congregated in thick piles where the vagaries of the tidal currents had gathered their remnants and deposited them on the sand. Razorshells live under the sand and are known as spoots in Scotland for the spouts of water they eject from their burrow entrances. By the low tide mark, the presence of their burrows can sometimes be identified as gentle depressions in the sand, but they are hard to detect and need an expert eye. They are curious shellfish, rarely seen alive because of their hidden existence where they feed by positioning an exit siphon above the sand surface to extract particles of organic matter from the sea. When disturbed, the razorshell uses its large muscular 'foot' to rapidly move deeper into the sediment.

I picked a razorshell up and examined its elongated shell. It was beautifully patterned and because it had only recently met its demise, the shell was burnished in an olive-green sheen, gently brushed with rippled lines. Over time, the half-shells lose their lustre. There were many razorshells littering the beach and I speculated that a recent storm had scoured them from their sandy homes, causing widespread mortality.

The tide was half-out on this part of the outer Dee Estuary known as the Point of Ayr, which is the northernmost point of mainland Wales, and where a lighthouse stands precariously between the high and low tide mark. The original lighthouse was built around 1776 after two ships were lost in the area and featured two lights, one which shone towards Llandudno and the other across the Dee Estuary. On the other side of the estuary lay the English coast of the Wirral, and beyond that, Birkenhead and Liverpool.

I ventured past the lighthouse and down towards the shoreline, where the strong wind whipped a blizzard of sand grains across the surface of the beach. Offshore, the brown sea churned and tears filled my eyes from the unrelenting blast of wind, which made it difficult to discern much detail through my binoculars. Lines of dark ducks bobbed in the water, disappearing and reappearing upon the tops of the swell in a stomach-heaving undulatory motion. The ducks were scoters, autumn and winter visitors from breeding grounds in Iceland, Norway, Sweden, Finland and northern Russia, although small numbers also nest in northern Scotland. By the shore edge, large groups of oystercatchers had gathered, most of whom were resting.

I headed back up the beach, stopping briefly by some rocks and pools near the lighthouse to lift stones in search of marine creatures lurking beneath. It quickly became apparent that, because of the wind, this wasn't the day for rock pooling, so instead I immersed myself within the large, rolling sand-dune system that lay beyond the upper shore. I followed some fox tracks in the sand but soon lost the trail and began to focus on the plant life instead. There was an abundance of sea-holly, a small bushy and prickly plant.

Despite the lateness of the season some of the sea-holly was still in flower, their wispy purple blossom looking like miniature thistle blooms. The jagged, frosty-blue and wax-stiff leaves of sea-holly are well adapted to cope with the harsh conditions of dunes, continually exposed to briny sea winds while the roots somehow eke out a parsimonious existence from the dry and nutrient poor substrate.

Sea-holly is patchily distributed along our coasts and is scarce in Scotland but more frequent in England and Wales. From the sixteenth to nineteenth centuries the roots of sea-holly were candied with sugar creating a sweet delicacy called 'eringo', which Colchester in Essex was famous for.

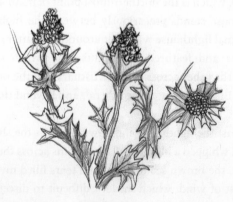

Sea Holly

It was especially popular with the elderly and was believed to have aphrodisiacal properties. The Elizabethan botanist, John Gerard, wrote that the candied roots were:

> exceedingly good to be given to old and aged people that are consumed and withered with age, and which want natural moisture: they are also good for other sorts of people, nourishing and restoring the aged, and amending the defects of nature in the younger.

Sea-holly is probably much scarcer nowadays than in the past because it was often hoicked out from the sand and shingle by beachgoers fearful of the prickly leaves catching their bare feet and ankles, and because it was once widely collected by horticulturalists for gardens, where it makes an attractive ornamental.

Interestingly, on the dunes were the fluffy seed-heads of another plant that had caught the attention of John Gerard several centuries ago. It was traveller's joy, so named because Gerard found it 'decking and adorning ways and hedges where people travel'. This is still true today and traveller's joy is prolific along railway embankments in London. A member of the clematis family, it is sometimes known as 'old-man's-beard' in reference to the long strands of wispy down once the seed has set.

The yellow flowering spikes of common evening primrose were still partially in bloom. Also known as evening star, the plant was introduced into Britain in the seventeenth century from North America and grown in gardens for its nut-flavoured roots which were boiled like parsnips. It has now become naturalised in many parts of Britain on waste ground, roadside verges and sand dunes. The flowers are rich in nectar and attract bees, butterflies, and moths, making it one of those non-natives which have no discernible negative impact on the environment. The seeds are the source of evening-primrose oil, which is believed to have medicinal properties in treating skin ailments and other disorders.

As I reluctantly left the dunes to continue my wildlife journey, I reflected upon our past reliance and intimate knowledge of wild plants as food and herbal treatments. At one time, humanity was in tune with nature and the environment, and herbal remedies would have been passed down from generation to generation, after having first been discovered through trial and error, and by watching the various types of plants and berries eaten by animals and birds.

This empathy with nature has now largely gone, which is the tragic loss of a fundamental bedrock of the human soul and a stark warning for the future. With habitats being destroyed all over the world, in particular our rainforests, there is the ever-present danger of valuable plant species with beneficial properties so far undiscovered being lost for good – whether it be for medicine or developing disease resistant crops for agriculture.

Chapter 22

A TIT THAT IS NOT A TIT & NATURE'S WILD CALLING

October 2022, Lancashire

Leighton Moss, near Carnforth in Lancashire, boasts the largest reed bed in northwest England and is home to scarce birds including bearded tits and marsh harriers. In my mind, it has always been one of those legendary natural havens in Britain, a place I have always wanted to visit but never had the opportunity to do so.

The day was overcast, rain threatened and the light was poor. The conditions for bird spotting were not ideal, but I have become much more relaxed nowadays when it comes to watching nature. When younger, it was all about seeing as much as possible and ticking-off species, now my attitude is more reflective and more about the simple appreciation of the environment. If I see something rare or unusual, then that is good, but it is not the be-all and end-all, and should never be so.

Thus, when I climbed an observation tower that overlooked the reedbeds, I did not even bother to scan the water with binoculars and instead soaked up the wild landscape, savouring the bigger picture of the overall environment. The reedbeds and pools were set in a shallow bowl in the landscape, bounded by gently raised wooded ground around. A short distance away, out of sight from the viewing platform, lay the vast expanse of Morecambe Bay, famous for its cockles and shrimps, and a sanctuary for waders, geese and ducks.

It did not take long for my curiosity to be aroused by the ducks on the water and I began to examine them more closely. Not only was the light poor, but most of the ducks were in their transformational eclipse plumage stage caused by the annual moult and the drakes were dowdy and lacking in brilliance. No matter, for there was a good mix of ducks, including scores of teal, gadwall, pintail, mallard and shovelers, which busily fed in the shallows of a lagoon. The shovelers were especially engaging as they busily swept their large shovel-shaped bills from side-to-side in the mud to sieve for small invertebrates and plant detritus.

Pintails are elegant and slender ducks with long pointy black tails and extended necks. They up-end continuously when feeding, their pin tails poking straight up into the air. It is a rare and declining breeder in Britain, nesting in places such as Orkney, the Hebrides and the Ouse Washes, and is principally a winter visitor where they exhibit a liking for grazing marshes, river floodplains and estuaries and sheltered coasts. In the Solent in Hampshire, the pintail has the local name of 'sea pheasant' because of the long tail.

I descended the tower and wandered the network of paths in this RSPB reserve, visiting some of the observation hides and enjoying more close encounters with ducks. Near one of the hides was a bird table with grit scattered on top, which was designed to attract bearded tits. During summer, bearded tits eat insects, but in autumn and winter they change their diet to reed seeds. The seeds are extremely tough, so the birds eat grit which aids the digestion process by grinding the hard husks into a digestible pulp.

Bearded Tits

The bearded tit is neither bearded nor a tit. It was originally thought to be a member of the more exotic parrotbill family, which are typically found in places such as Nepal and Mongolia. However, further research has revealed they have the accolade of belonging to their own distinctive family. Another name for the bird is the bearded reedling, which is more appropriate, although moustached reedling would be even more apt, for the 'beard' of the male is more akin to a moustache. Despite the misnomers that surround the bird, it is certainly a most attractive species, especially the male with his blue-grey head, russet upperparts and long tail.

The ability to change their diet to reed seeds negates the need to migrate to warmer climes in winter, although bearded tits are extremely vulnerable to prolonged cold spells when the population can plummet. However, they are prolific breeders and numbers usually bounce back quickly. As a reed bed specialist, they have evolved a remarkable means of colonising new areas by undergoing periodic 'eruptions' in autumn where small flocks suddenly take to the air from their home reedbed and go exploring pastures new, sometimes for considerable distances. Reed beds are scattered habitats and essentially isolated islands in the landscape, and these eruptive movements enable the colonisation of new areas, replenish existing colonies in other places, and no doubt help reinvigorate the gene pool in the process.

I had visited several other reedbeds in England and Wales during my wildlife journey where bearded tits occurred but had never caught sight of one. Leighton Moss drew a similar blank. They are birds that like to lurk in the depths of the reeds and live their secret lives largely under wraps.

On walking the boardwalks and other paths through the reserve, the reeds themselves became the focus of my attention. The reedbed environment is extraordinary and home to many specialised creatures including bitterns, reed warblers, marsh harriers, and, of course, bearded tits. These spectacular species make it is easy to ignore the very building block of their existence – the reeds. The arrangement of the stiff, flat, and tapered leaves of the reeds at Leighton Moss had a beguiling artistic element because they all pointed in the direction of the wind like tiers of elongated flags. On staring into the reeds with my eyes, my focus became fudged and confused, creating a hypnotic effect that giddied the mind.

There are less than a thousand reedbeds in Britain and only around 50 are big enough to support bitterns, heron-like birds which need at least 20 hectares to ensure a viable population. In Britain, the reed has the

Bittern & Reed Beds, Leighton Moss

distinction of being the tallest non-woody native plant. It can also tolerate brackish and even polluted waters. In autumn, reeds take on a slightly purple hue as the seeds develop. In winter, the heads are fluffy and reed stems die-off, giving the familiar straw-coloured appearance. The old reeds eventually fall to the ground, and at Leighton Moss, reserve managers regularly cut and rake large areas to prevent the reed litter turning to peat and drying out the beds.

As a result, reedbeds are inherently unstable environments and when left to their own devices will become invaded by willow scrub and other trees and turn into damp woodland. In essence, it is nature's way of creating new habitat, but it would also seem to be the road to extinction for freshwater reedbeds, something fortunately avoided over the millennia. Part of the reason may be because reedbeds have been managed by people from the earliest times, being cut and harvested for thatching material and other purposes; and beavers would have continually cut new watery channels through their vast expanses. Reeds are the ultimate colonisers, quickly appearing on new bodies of freshwater, further aiding their success.

On a dry section of path by one of the Leighton Moss reedbeds, I discovered a duo of shaggy inkcap mushrooms oozing glistening black ink from their caps. In the past, inkcaps were used to make writing ink by mixing the dark liquid from the mushrooms with a little water and some cloves, and then heating it. This process helped fix the ink and stopped it from fading or running when used.

From Leighton Moss, I ventured to nearby Morecambe Bay, which holds the largest expanse of sand and intertidal mudflats in Britain. The bay is all encompassing, stretching from southwest Cumbria in the north to Fleetwood in Lancashire in the south, taking in coastal towns such as Grange-over-Sands, Morecambe and Heysham. The mud draws in over a quarter of a million ducks, geese and wading birds each winter, including curlews, dunlins, godwits, knots and oystercatchers to forage upon the abundant cockles, shrimps, lugworms and other marine invertebrates. There are more oystercatchers at Morecambe Bay than any other estuary in Britain.

The pancake-flat landscape had an air of welcome familiarity, which I think stemmed from my recent visit to The Wash in Lincolnshire. From an observation hide nestled by a muddy creek, shelduck, shovelers and teal busily fed, whilst on a small mud island in a lagoon, a large roost of redshanks gently slumbered. Dusk was approaching and the wild geese were on the move, excitedly calling and honking to one another as they settled on a nearby saltmarsh on whiffling wings. This was a beckoning cry, so mesmerising that I could have lingered here forever, bound within the warm embrace of nature's wild calling and reluctant to relinquish its bewitching hold.

Chapter 23

FABULOUS FUNGI & DILIGENT GARDENERS

November 2022, County Durham

My soul is awakened, my spirit is soaring
And carried aloft on the wings of the breeze;
For above and around me the wild wind is roaring,
Arousing to rapture the earth and the seas.
The long withered grass in the sunshine is glancing,
The bare trees are tossing their branches on high;
The dead leaves beneath them are merrily dancing,
The white clouds are scudding across the blue sky.
I wish I could see how the ocean is lashing
The foam of its billows to whirlwinds of spray;
I wish I could see how its proud waves are dashing,
And hear the wild roar of their thunder to-day!

'Lines Composed in a Wood on a Windy Day',
by Anne Brontë

It was autumn in the wild wood of Hamsterley Forest. The ground was thick with fallen leaves, a multi-coloured carpet that rustled and yielded under my gentle footfall. With cupped hands, I scooped a ragged bundle of leaves that were already beginning to decompose, and within this handful of death was the deliverance of new life. In time, these leaves will transform into leaf mould that will return valuable nutrients back to the soil. As I placed the claggy clump back onto the ground, I gently teased apart some of the leaf litter, revealing tiny millipedes and a solitary pink, wriggling earthworm.

When the grip of winter comes, this comfort blanket will insulate against the worst excesses and provide a protective haven for micro-creatures that may otherwise succumb if exposed to the full cold. When the ground is frosted hard, blackbirds will seek out such areas of woodland, turning over the leaves with quick flicks of the beak in search of the hidden plenitude below.

Fly Agaric Toadstools

A smouldering ember glowed from the base of a nearby birch – a group of three fly agaric toadstools with their scarlet caps frosted with white. The speed a fly agaric grows is astonishing, several centimetres in height per day during their initial emergence from the ground – first appearing as a small dome-like protuberance, bright red with a sprinkling of white-flaked spots, then the stalk, followed by the unfurling of the cap like a burnished, red umbrella. On searching more closely, I found several more clusters of fly agarics, which decorated the woodland floor as if part of a picture-book scene from a fairy tale.

The umbrella caps of toadstools and mushrooms so obvious in autumn, are fleeting ghosts in the wind that appear for only a short time. They are the fruiting bodies designed to produce and distribute spores, and quickly wither once they have done their job. While not visible for most of the year, fungi are still there, working their quiet magic whether it be in the soil or in decaying wood, or even in the air that we breathe. Fungi are everywhere, and without them our world would lack heart, for they aid growth of trees through mutually-beneficial relationships, drive organic decomposition, recycle nutrients back into the soil, and touch our lives in so many other diverse ways, including the yeasts that give us our daily bread, and for crucial medicines such as penicillin.

The fly agaric is closely associated with birch and pine trees in a symbiotic relationship where its sprawling underground threads (collectively known as mycelium) aid tree roots in absorbing minerals from the soil. In return, the fly agarics gain nutrients the tree has generated.

Excited by my discovery, I carefully searched the woodland floor for other fungi and it was not long before a nugget of gold shone out before me. It was yellow stagshorn, a true citron gem, with a small and intricate branched form that is a million miles away from the traditional shape of a toadstool. Their beauty of form and brightness of colour was beguiling and it was tremendously fulfilling to be down at eye level on the woodland floor. This was like entering a different world, with a rich, heady aroma of leaf mould enveloping my senses, almost as if the very essence of the earth was filling my lungs.

I rose to my feet and wandered over to an old, tumbled tree trunk, so decomposed it was hard to identify, although it may have been an oak or an elm. A mere shadow of its former self, the fallen leviathan was a brooding hulk, its remnant skeletal branches pointing heavenwards as if in a last-ditch plea for salvation. I ran my hands over a section of the trunk and felt the pulse of life within. There were numerous tiny pinprick holes made by boring insects and other invertebrates. This was a place for invertebrates to feed, seek shelter and to lay eggs – and a place, too, for woodpeckers to probe and inspect with eager anticipation.

It was the fungi that was the overwhelming draw of this decayed giant and I carefully circled the trunk, mentally cataloguing different types. An elliptical, vibrant scar of wrinkled crust fungus coated one section in a creeping encrustation of grey and yellow, tinged with orange. There were also olive oysterlings, which had the more typical toadstool appearance, with greenish caps and small stalks that curved out from the tree in tiers. The more I looked, the more was revealed, including the miniscule orange specks of coral spot fungus and the marginally larger yellow discs of lemon disco. Dark, charcoal rubber-like blobs, coated part of the trunk, which were sticky to the touch. This was black bulgar, a most unusual-looking fungus, which is also known as bachelor's buttons or rubber buttons. In North America, it is sometimes referred to as black jelly drops, or poor man's liquorice (although it is not edible).

This long-dead tree was an island of life and a provider of new opportunity, a nature reserve in miniature. I savoured once more the wonderful names of these fungi – lemon disco and olive oysterling, black bulgar and coral spot – as poetic and uplifting as the vibrancy they brought to this wood. The tree was a pedestal for the immense variety of fungi in our environment, ranging from familiar types such as toadstools to others that are club or bracket shaped, or form encrusting moulds. Such diversity in shape and form is matched by the brilliant array of colours fungi exhibit, including every shade of red imaginable, ochres, yellows and tints of orange.

As I explored the wood, there were many fungi that defied my identification abilities, which made me wish I was more knowledgeable. Although there were some familiar exceptions, including a puffball, which when I gently squeezed with my fingers, released a powder-puff of spores that swirled away in the breeze like billowing smoke.

Fungi are both compelling and frustrating: the former because of their infinite beauty and variety, the latter because they are often incredibly difficult to identify, even for experts. The number of species of fungi in Britain is immense, around 15,000 different types, and no doubt there are many more that have yet to be discovered.

Managed by Forestry England, Hamsterley Forest is the largest area of commercial plantation in County Durham, and is situated in the valley of the Bedburn Beck, which drains the eastern tip of the upland ridge between Teesdale and Weardale by the edge of the North Pennines. It was planted after the First World War to help replenish Britain's depleted timber stocks, and while it comprises principally of Sitka spruce, there is also Scots pine and larch, as well as good areas of deciduous woodland, meadow and parkland. Scarce wood ants prosper in the forest, as do many different types of butterfly, including rarities such as the holly blue and high brown fritillary.

Despite being November, the damp air was warm, aiding the decomposition processes that were going on all around me. A party of jays screeched somewhere in the distance, and were most probably busy collecting and hoarding beech mast and acorns from the woodland, filling their throats to engorgement.

Jay & Acorns

I wandered farther into the forest, engrossed by the fungi all around. My eyes were drawn to a tuft of exquisite bonnet mushrooms on a tree stump, their grey caps scored with radiating grooves. I thought initially they were common bonnets, but on looking closer was not so sure. I took a photograph, so that I could identify them more accurately later using a fungi guidebook. The research proved inconclusive and I remained uncertain of the species. This little cluster of bonnets was a mystery of the forest, a secret of the wild, and a homage to the vast diversity of nature that lives around us.

Chapter 24

BARNACLE GEESE & THE SECRETS OF
THE SALTMARSH

January 2023, Cumbria

The ice crunched under my feet but the mud beneath was frozen hard, creating an impenetrable crust that failed to yield. Despite the brackish influence of the tide, a prolonged period of deep frost had hardened the mudflats of the inner Solway Firth in northern Cumbria.

The concentration of salt in the waters of the estuarine channel of the River Eden by the village of Bowness-on-Solway was clearly too weak to have stemmed the impact of severe frost. There was barely a whisper of wind and a brittle winter sun brimmed the horizon. Ice crystals on the shore glinted under the sunbeams and the call of geese drifted across the still air, a haunting sound that is the essence of winter and a wild enchantment from the north.

I had last visited the inner Solway in March 2021 as the starting point for my book *A Scottish Wildlife Odyssey*, and the saltmarshes, or merse, at Caerlaverock, which was not too far away on the north shore in Dumfries-shire, had immediately overwhelmed me by its vastness and the bustle of life held within. In this little corner of southwest Scotland, geese honked, curlews trilled and redshanks piped, instilling memories that are forever ingrained.

The saltmarshes around Bowness-on-Solway may not hold the grandeur of Caerlaverock, but nonetheless feature the same captivating wild calling of nature and the intoxicant aroma of the coast. I wandered over the short grasses of the saltmarsh on the upper shore and ventured down onto the frozen mud, where across a narrow sliver of mirror-like water lay the Scottish shore. In the distance, the distinctive whaleback of Criffel, a 570 m high hill in Kirkcudbrightshire, broke the skyline. The gentle current of the Eden drifted loose groups of wigeon out towards the firth, who were cleverly using the flow as an energy-efficient means of moving from one area to another. When the tide turns, they will sweep back upriver again to forage in pastures new.

A large flock of lapwings roosted on a tidal mudbank, intermittently swirling into the air before quickly settling again. A sweep of my binoculars revealed a congregation of oystercatchers on another tidal bank, as well as many curlews and redshanks. By a small winding channel on the middle shore, the encrusted ice formed intricate patterns that sparkled under the watery morning sun.

Barnacle Goose

Then the noise – that special noise – the high-pitched clamouring of a skein of barnacle geese sweeping overhead in a V-formation, their dark bodies and pale faces caught in perfect vision by the clear winter light as they headed westwards in a purposeful flight. Another gaggle of geese – this time greylags – etched the sky, before making a tight turn over a large frozen pool on the saltmarsh. They wheeled round again as if inspecting the ice-covered pool as a place for settling. The ice was a discouragement, and they rose in the air, honking in agitation as they disappeared over the horizon.

The thrill of glimpsing wild geese invariably sends tingles of excitement coursing down my spine. I am not sure why this should be so, but I think it is down to the combination of geese and the empty landscape merging as a single entity, creating a wonderful wildness that stirs the heart like few other natural experiences can.

Greylag geese are common, both as winter migrant arrivals and resident breeders, while barnacle geese are much scarcer with the Solway area representing a crucially important wintering site. The entire breeding population of the Svalbard archipelago off northern Norway winters on the Solway, making its saltmarshes, mudflats and surrounding fields of immense conservation importance.

A separate population of barnacle geese breed in Greenland, wintering in northern and western parts of Scotland, from Orkney down through the Hebrides to Islay, and across into Ireland. Another group nest on Novaya Zemlya and adjacent areas in northern Russia, wintering in the Netherlands. In the mid-1970s, some of these Russian birds established separate breeding populations on islands in the Baltic.

Bird Flu has taken a terrible toll on Solway barnacle goose numbers, with over a third lost during the winter of 2021/22. Thankfully, the subsequent breeding season was good, and mortalities during the winter of 2022/23 were low (although the wintering population on Islay suffered badly during that same period). The virus is part of the cruel hand of nature, yet the robustness of life always seems to shine through. Hopefully, in the years to come, numbers will recover to former levels, and the evocative calls of the wild geese will continue to drift across the saltmarshes of the Solway.

I returned to the upper shore and sat on a grassy hummock surrounded by the watery channels and dark pools that characterise the saltmarsh. The Solway wetlands of Cumbria are hugely important for geese and wintering wading birds because of abundant food sources. In spring, curlews, redshanks and lapwings nest in nearby damp meadows, while skylarks soar overhead.

The mudflats hold mind-boggling quantities of invertebrates – there may be as many as 20,000 burying amphipods (small, shrimp-like crustaceans) and 200,000 miniscule mud snails per square metre of sediment.

Wading birds congregate in large numbers to take advantage of this prolific larder, as do flatfish like flounders, dabs and soles. Molluscs are similarly abundant, including tellins, peppery furrow shells and cockles. Lugworms, ragworms and a range of smaller worm species thrive in the sediment.

Despite the plethora of diversity, it is a challenging environment with the sand bars and mud banks constantly shifting due to strong tidal streams and wave action. The Solway is a highly dynamic environment where erosion and deposition occur together. This is a place of life and death, yet where the riches of the shallow waters always shine through.

Lugworm

Farther inland from the saltmarsh, raised mires have formed in hollows left behind by retreating glaciers. The flooded hollows were initially colonised by sedges and reeds, followed by carpets of vibrant sphagnum moss. The dead moss turned to peat over time, while the continuing progression of living moss slowly rose above the level of the surrounding land. The resultant patchwork of wet areas and drier hummocks has created a lowland bog that is home to plants like sundews and bog asphodel. Insects that occur include damselflies and dragonflies, as well as the rare marsh fritillary butterfly which was reintroduced after becoming extinct in the area in 1991. Human activity has similarly shaped the landscape; the remains of the Roman fort of Maia lie at the western end of Hadrian's Wall by Bowness-on-Solway, while in the twelfth and thirteenth centuries, Cistercian monks managed the land to create improved grazing for sheep.

From my perch on the saltmarsh hummock, I brushed my fingers across the short-cropped grass. Grasses are ubiquitous, yet their overwhelming ecological importance is understated. The predominate species here was common saltmarsh grass, a pioneering plant that can withstand the regular inundation of the brackish tide. It is a hardy pioneer, living its existence quite literally on the edge and helping to bind and trap sediment in the precarious zone between land and water. A range of other saline tolerant plants inhabit saltmarshes including sea milkwort, marsh samphire and scurvygrass. When these plants die, rather than decomposing and releasing their carbon into the atmosphere, they become buried in the mud. As the sediment gradually builds, further layers of vegetation become buried, locking up carbon in the mud and ensuring that saltmarshes act as important 'carbon sinks'. Unfortunately, a non-native species, cord grass, has also taken hold in many parts of the Solway, which has the potential to upset the delicate ecological balance and physical structure of the saltmarshes in the area.

I wondered whether the skein of barnacle geese that had flown overhead earlier in the morning had settled in a nearby field. *It would be good to get a closer view of them*, I thought, so, I followed the small shore road towards the hamlet of Cardurnock and soon, I spotted the geese in a field in front of a cluster of communication towers. I crept up to a low hawthorn hedge by the field margin and watched the grazing geese through my binoculars. Barnacles are undeniably attractive small geese, with their black crowns and necks, offset by a creamy face and a bill that is noticeably smaller compared to many other types of goose. There were about 50 barnacle geese in the flock and they grazed contentedly, slowing moving from one end of the field to the other.

Leaving the geese to graze in peace, I ventured to a vantage point overlooking the nearby estuary of the River Wampool by the small settlement of Anthorn. It was a peaceful spot and on one mudbank in the river channel a large flock of golden plovers roosted, their bills tucked under their wings for warmth. Many of the plovers were resting on just one leg with the other raised into the belly, another ploy many waders use to conserve heat. Golden plovers have plaintive calls that sound like the voices of lost souls carried in the wind.

On slender, slow flapping wings, a hunting short-eared owl ghosted into view over the marsh, veering and stalling, its head pointing downwards in rapt concentration. It gained height before gently gliding down, the piercing yellow eyes in its round face constantly scanning the ground for field voles. The wings flapped several more strokes, followed by a short glide, then another flurry of easy flapping before descending to the shoreside edge of the marsh.

While short-eared owls hunt mainly at night, they are unusual in that they will also do so during the day. Some short-eared owls are resident and breed sporadically in the Pennines and the hills and moors of Scotland. Many others are winter visitors, arriving here from Scandinavia and beyond. The ornithologist, Thomas Coward, wrote that these migrating owls 'feed upon other avian travellers, capturing them as they fly on misty nights in the glare from lighthouses'.

Short-eared Owl

Short-eared owls' 'ears' are not ears at all but instead two little feathery tufts on top of the head. Their most likely purpose is to enhance camouflage by breaking up the outline of the head. They may also be utilised for communication or signalling purposes – for example a startled owl will raise its tufts, much in the same way as we might use our eyebrows.

As I was about to depart, a snipe whirled-up into the air before quickly diving down and disappearing into a narrow muddy channel between the grass swards. Although out of sight, I mentally pictured the snipe probing its bill into the darkest corners of this fissure in the saltmarsh, seeking out worms and the other bountiful life that lay within the wild riches of the Solway.

Chapter 25

A BORDER DIVIDE & THE PHANTOM OF THE FOREST

January 2023, Northumberland

With one leg in Scotland and the other firmly planted in England, I straddled the border line high on the desolate and frozen expanse of Deadwater Fell, a hill of the Cheviots located a mere stone's throw from the source of the River North Tyne. The rolling fells and mosses were carpeted in a thin veneer of snow that glittered in the early afternoon sun. The landscape was stark and empty, although the hand of humanity prevailed in the form of sheep grazing and the network of forestry plantations that patchworked the hills.

I find border boundaries intriguing, which made me ponder: *'Why was the demarcation line here?'* On examining my map with cold-numbed fingers, it was apparent that topographically this was a watershed, with the burns that tumbled down from the Scottish side flowing into the River Esk, which empties into the inner reaches of the Solway Firth by Gretna. The nearby early trickling of the North Tyne on the Northumberland side fills the Kielder Water reservoir in the other direction and converges with the South Tyne near Hexham to create the River Tyne, which then follows an easterly course to spill out into the North Sea at Newcastle. Thus, despite the apparent uniformity of the upland landscape, there is a distinctive geographic divide, although the delineation of the actual border is, of course, entirely rooted in human history and conflict.

The temperature was sub-zero, making it a harsh wintery landscape for wildlife to eke out a living. In summer, meadow pipits abound among grass tussocks and skylarks sprinkle their melodious songs down upon the fells and moors. In winter, many birds abandon these uplands and much other life lies low, waiting for the first warming glimmers of spring.

Earlier that day, I had explored the vast expanse of the nearby Kielder Forest in Northumberland. Covering 65,000 hectares, Kielder Forest is the largest forestry plantation in Northumberland and Kielder Water the largest man-made reservoir (by capacity) in Europe. Starting at the Bakethin Nature Reserve, near the village of Kielder at the far north end of the Kielder Water, I followed a track by the water's edge. Initially, this was a narrow river strip comprising the early stages of the North Tyne, but it soon transformed into the enclosed basin of Bakethin Reservoir and then opened out into the vastness of Kielder Water. Bakethin was set aside as a nature reserve in 1979 when Kielder Dam was constructed. The reserve covers 140 hectares with a diverse range of habitats including open water, wetlands and woodlands.

Soft snow crumpled under my footfall as I passed under a high stone bridge where icicles hung precariously from the parapets. A robin perched on the branch of a small birch ahead and eyed me curiously. I stopped and took some photographs of the redbreast, who swooped down to the ground and then fluttered back up to the birch again. Robins are among our most endearing birds, yet behind a robin's gentle façade lies a bit of a bruiser.

Robin, Bakethin Reservoir

Both sexes are territorial, the male particularly so, and should another male alight on his patch, then with feathers ruffled and wings drooped he will do everything in his power to see off the unwelcome intruder. Usually, it is all about threat and posture with both males squaring up to each other with necks outstretched, showing off their vibrant red breasts.

A vicious chase will often ensue, as one bird pursues the other in short darting flights, before intermittently stopping to face up to each other again. Often this is enough to settle the dispute, but sometimes a furious fighting bout will result, with one robin pinning down the other in a frenzy of aggression. Occasionally, one of the combatants will get killed in the unseemly brawl.

Such aggressive behaviour may seem over-the-top, but for a robin its territory is of all-consuming importance, for it provides an exclusive food source during the lean days of winter and an area to raise young during spring and summer.

As I continued along the snowy track, I scanned the air above in the hope of glimpsing a goshawk. Kielder Forest is a stronghold for these spectacular phantoms of the forest, and despite the earliness of the season, both sexes often begin to engage in their spectacular aerial courtship displays in late January. The display sometimes consists of a repetition of deep plunges with wings beating slowly, followed by a steep rise where the wings are held tight against the body. Despite my constant scanning above the tops of the thick swathes of spruces, the azure sky remained frustratingly empty and devoid of goshawks.

Goshawk

As I walked on, memories flooded back from several years before when Forestry Commission Scotland (as it was known then) invited me to participate in a goshawk chick leg-ringing session at a site a short distance over the border near Bonchester Bridge. An article I wrote at the time for *The Scotsman* noted:

> We carefully made our way on foot into a remote forest until we came upon a more open part of the wood. Here, near the top of a pine tree we glimpsed the goshawk nest, a large bulky structure of branches and twigs that was perhaps a metre deep.
>
> On the ground radiating several yards out from the tree were the tell-tale signs of occupancy in the form of droppings that the young birds had squirted out from the nest. A careful search of the ground also revealed the remains of prey items, including the breastbone of a pigeon; the deep notches in its sternum a sure sign of the power of a goshawk's beak. With the aid of special tree climbing boots and equipment, the tree was ascended by one of ringers, who gently lowered each of the three chicks in a bag down to the ground. Numbered and coloured rings were carefully secured around the legs of each bird and the youngsters were weighed and measured. There were two females and a male. Moulted adult feathers were also collected from around the nest which will later be analysed and recorded into a DNA database. All these actions have the potential to provide invaluable information on the movements of our goshawks and help provide crucial evidence in cases of illegal persecution.

It was a truly special experience and I still recall with clarity the fierce defiance of the yellow-eyed goshawk chicks. The leg-ringing and DNA monitoring were important because the goshawk is widely persecuted even to this day. In the past, the sublime hunting skills of the goshawk were cherished in falconry and in hierarchal terms it was known as the yeoman's hawk. It is also a bird shrouded in mystery and intrigue, and there is still a great deal of confusion over its former historical status as a breeding bird in Britain. What is certain is that a combination of deforestation and persecution had virtually exterminated the goshawk as a native breeder by the late nineteenth century. From the late 1960s onwards, breeding became more regular due to new birds arriving on the scene, mainly from deliberate releases by falconers and from escaped birds. The number of breeding pairs has steadily built up since then, but it is still a scarce bird of prey.

While there is no doubt the goshawk is a formidable predator that will sometimes take game birds, a more conciliatory view of the goshawk should be adopted by landowners still fearful of its presence, for it eats a wide range of other prey too, including creatures many estates might regard as pests such as crows, pigeons, grey squirrels and rabbits. More to the point, persecution is illegal.

On my return journey back up Kielder Water, I observed several buzzards soaring high in the sky. While the goshawk still retains a somewhat tenuous existence, the buzzard is a bird of prey that has experienced a phenomenal recovery in recent decades after it too had previously suffered from intense persecution. It is now probably our commonest bird of prey and the astonishing recovery in numbers is mainly due to a dramatic fall in persecution in recent decades aided by legal protection afforded by the Wildlife and Countryside Act 1981.

While the hand of the law is a major influence, it is fair to say that this reduced persecution has been helped to a significant degree by a more enlightened attitude towards our environment – a recognition that all life is important and that people and nature can coexist in mutual harmony. The bounce-back has been helped by the buzzard's ability to exploit a wide variety of habitats from mountain, moor and farmland to coastal areas and the edges of suburbia. The buzzard is an adaptable predator; it will take mammals up to the size of a small rabbit, but beetles are also hunted and it will even devour earthworms. Countryside verges are good places for it to scavenge for road-kill animals or to hunt for mice and voles. Indeed, any car trip in the country will usually bring at least one sighting of a buzzard, with its penchant for prominent roadside perches resulting in the buzzard being known as the 'telegraph pole eagle' in some parts of the country.

As I neared my starting point by Kielder village, I stopped by a small frozen pond where the sun's rays filtered through the straggly birches that encircled it. A robin warbled from nearby, a soft and gentle song with a hint of melancholy. Behind that cloak of tranquillity, I knew, lay a streak of aggression and the robin would be watching carefully for any interloper that dared impinge upon its territory. It sang a few more notes, and as it did so, I pulled my jacket collar up for extra warmth and slipped away under the comfort blanket of the sun's diminishing winter rays.

Chapter 26

A GOOSE ENIGMA & GREY-DRIPPED LICHENS

January 2023, North Lanarkshire

There is something mystical about winter sunlight in Scotland because the softness of the luminescence against the withered grass, bracken and heather conjures an orange-tinted glow to the landscape, especially in those special moments prior to sunset.

In glens and straths this unveils a remarkable panorama where the lower altitude parts of the land are cloaked in shade, while the hill slopes and tops have a copper-burnished incandescence, resulting in a stark contrast between darkness and light as if reflecting upon the despair of winter and the hope of spring. Such magical light deliverance was to the fore on this bog in North Lanarkshire. The sun hung low in an azure sky, painting the surrounding open ground in an artistic canvas of ochre and amber.

Far to the north lay the snow-capped peaks of Ben Vorlich and Stuc a' Chroin by Loch Earn, but such was the clarity of the air it seemed as if they were much closer. In many ways, everything is within touching distance in Scotland. From the nearby Ochil Hills, it is possible to see simultaneously the Isle of May in the outer Firth of Forth in the east and the rocky, two-peaked top of the Cobbler above Loch Long in the west, which is a popular hill for walkers.

At first glance, bogs appear bleak – flat and featureless with a uniformity that dulls the mind. Yet, as with most initial impressions, whether with people or landscapes, this is a mere illusion and beauty is invariably more than skin deep. And it does not take much delving to appreciate the full riches held within this landscape. With bogs, this is an allure not without risk, and on tentatively striking out across the marshy ground, I sank knee deep into a hidden damp flush, my boots filling with icy-cold water. It was a struggle to pull free from the clawing grip of this peaty entrapment, and once I had done so, it dawned on me that this was an environment to be treated with respect and caution.

Fannyside Muir is a lowland raised bog that lies between the towns of Falkirk and Cumbernauld in central Scotland. The bog is situated in an area of upland ground known as the Slamannan Plateau, approximately 170 m above sea level. The aspect of the plateau is best gauged when seen from the Inner Forth estuary, where a distinct escarpment can be seen breaking the skyline to the south. The plateau features a scattering of raised bogs and is interspersed with farms for grazing sheep and cattle.

The Slamannan Plateau has lost half of its original peatland due to the impact of drainage for peat extraction, mining, afforestation, overgrazing and other human activity. Most of the remaining areas of bog are in a degraded state. On a wider scale, 96 per cent of lowland raised bogs have been lost in Scotland, a tragic demise because they are home to unique aggregations of life and act as important carbon stores in the battle against climate change. There are many specialised bog invertebrate species, including the tiny bog pseudoscorpion and the window-winged sedge. The large heath butterfly is another bog dependent species, requiring areas of cotton-grass to thrive.

Raised bogs are created where the rate of accumulation of plant debris exceed decay, so that the resultant build-up of peat elevates the bog surface to form a gently rounded dome, which creates a huge damp sponge consisting of sphagnum and other mosses and vegetation. Some peat bogs are around 9,500 years old and are important natural features of the landscape.

To address the dire situation of bog loss, the Falkirk Lowland Raised Bog Restoration Project was set up by conservationists to focus on restoring nine bogs in the Slamannan Plateau area, including scrub clearance and the building of dams and bunds to trap water to help the bogs regain their former integrity. By restoring these remaining remnants of bog and peatland, it is hoped to enhance important stepping-stone bog habitats linking the north of the plateau to the south. It will, of course be a slow process. Sphagnum moss is the key peatland creation species due to its decomposition and peat accumulation progresses at a rate of only 1 mm per year when a bog is active.

Judging by the watery immersion I had just experienced, such work was clearly bearing fruit. I decided against attempting to venture out over the bog once more and opted instead to follow a small road by its margin to gain a flavour of the aura of the landscape. Interesting species on the bog in summer include the emperor moth and a type of ground beetle closely associated with sphagnum. In winter, it is taiga bean geese – one of Scotland's rarest migratory birds – which inspires and the hope of glimpsing them was the principal reason for my visit to the plateau.

The taiga bean goose is an enigma. The goose was probably widespread as a winter visitor to Scotland during the nineteenth century, and in the first half of the twentieth century, the stronghold was around the Dee Marshes at Castle Douglas in southwest Scotland. However, numbers there gradually dwindled and the site was abandoned by the 1980s. During this period, the flock began to regularly visit the Slamannan Plateau and they still do so to this day. The number of geese that arrive each year is small – around 250 birds – and they belong to a group that nest in Sweden. There are two species of bean goose in the Western Palaearctic – the taiga bean goose from the boreal forests of Scandinavia and Russia, and the tundra bean goose, which is associated with more open, tundra habitats farther north.

Taiga Bean Goose, Ben Vorlich & Stue à Choin, Fannyside Muir

The only other wintering population of taiga bean goose in Britain was formerly associated with the Yare Valley in Norfolk, but it is virtually non-existent nowadays due to a phenomenon known as 'short-stopping'. Winters are no longer sufficiently cold and hard to justify crossing the North Sea to East Anglia from other wintering grounds in the Low Countries, the birds opting to stay on the near continent throughout the winter.

Taiga bean geese at Slamannan graze in the surrounding fields during the day and are vulnerable to disturbance, so I kept to country lanes, scanning open areas of the countryside carefully with my binoculars. The search proved fruitless, and when not too far from Cumbernauld, I discovered a stretch of woodland which I struck into as a welcome diversion from the disheartening lack of geese. After a while a lone birch richly adorned with lichens loomed before me. The surrounding trees were devoid of lichens and it was a mystery why this birch was so richly endowed when the others were not.

I caressed this thick flush of grey-dripped lichens, marvelling at their intricate shape and form, creating a wondrous silvery shroud that glinted under the rays of sunshine that filtered through the thick tangle of branches in the woodland. The predomnant type was 'old man's beard' which hung in thick tassels, but there were several other more compact lichens. As I examined these lichens, it was difficult to get my head around their complex biology.

Old Man's Beard Lichen

Rather than one organism, lichens consist of a symbiotic association of fungi and algae, or sometimes with cyanobacteria, which is a type of blue-green algae. These composite organisms work in a mutually-beneficial partnership where the fungus gleans nourishment from the photosynthetic properties of the alga (or cyanobacterium), while the alga gains protective shelter and support from the fungus, ensuring optimal living conditions. In effect, lichens are mini ecosystems.

Lichens are one of the bedrocks of the natural environment and even occur in the harshest environments including Arctic tundra, mountain tops, hot dry deserts and rocky coasts. It is in woodland where lichens come to the fore, benefiting wildlife by providing shelter for invertebrates, which in turn are feasted upon by a range of other creatures, including birds such as tits and treecreepers. Many birds use lichens as nesting material during spring and summer. Lichens are useful indicators of air quality, thriving in places where the atmosphere is clean and pure, which was possibly the reason why lichens were so scarce on the other trees in this central Scotland woodland, given the proximity of urban areas.

Dusk was fast approaching and the last opportunity to view taiga bean geese lay in a nearby loch where they often roost on the surrounding mosses. I ventured to the shore edge and sat by a small alder. The loch was completely covered in ice, the surface of which was ruffled and scarred by the subtle movement of the water as it froze. I suspected the ice would discourage the geese from roosting in the area, but nonetheless decided to linger. A lone crow perched in a nearby birch and a pair of red grouse swept by in a low flight close to the shore edge. I was surprised to see the grouse, imagining them to be more birds of hill areas, but heather is abundant in the surrounding bogs and mosses which grouse like to eat.

A few herring gulls circled above as the orange-glowed sun slipped below the trees on the far side of the loch. A raven flew over uttering its distinctive 'cronk, cronk' call. The temperature fell rapidly with the diminishment of the sun and there was still no sight nor sound of geese. I waited for a while longer in this frozen-aired cloak of darkness, ears straining to detect the calls of an incoming skein. But the dark night air remained stubbornly still and silent apart from the soft crackle of ice as it gently shifted by the shore edge.

Chapter 27

THREE-TOED WADERS & SHELLFISH ANTIQUARIES

February 2023, Fife

On pattering feet, the sanderlings dodged in amongst the surf, following the flow of the sea as it receded and quickly retreating up the beach again as the rolling water surged back. Up and down the shore at Largo Bay they skipped, snapping up tiny crustaceans and worms that had been revealed by the crashing waves.

They were like confetti in the wind, dancing and jigging, and spiralling momentarily up into the air on quick-flashed wings. Unusually for a bird, sanderlings lack a hind toe, which is an adaptation that enables them to run rapidly on sand. It does, however, make the birds unstable on their feet when the wind blows, often getting tumbled sideways before regaining poise and balance once more.

Sanderlings are winter visitors to Scotland, hailing from breeding grounds in Greenland. Their presence on the wide expanses of Largo Bay in the Firth of Forth was a telling reminder of Scotland's international importance for vulnerable wader populations.

Sanderlings

When I examined the pearly-plumaged sanderlings through my binoculars, it was discernible that several of the birds sported coloured leg rings. This was something I had noticed on previous visits to Largo Bay. I did some research and it transpired that these birds had been ringed on Sanday in Orkney a few years previously in spring as they made their way back to their breeding grounds in Greenland. Sanday is an important stopping-over point during migration, where the sanderlings feed upon the rich supply of fly larvae found in rotting seaweed banks.

Leg-ringing plays a vital role in enhancing our knowledge of birds like sanderlings and the migratory movements they undertake. The greater our understanding of birds' behaviours and ecology, the better we can protect them and ensure effective conservation strategies. Ringing has revealed that the Largo Bay sanderlings belong to a tribe that are very site faithful, returning to this part of the Forth each year and no doubt breeding in the same favoured location in Greenland.

It was a blustery day, with the wind blowing strong from the west creating a seemingly never-ending procession of rollers crashing upon the beach. I left the sanderlings to their hopping, skipping and jumping by the shore edge and wandered over to the strandline on the upper beach. Mounds of slowly decaying kelp and other seaweeds had accumulated, and just as how such rotting masses provide a rich larder for sanderlings when passing through Orkney, so too does it provide a bountiful source of food at Largo Bay for other types of bird.

A flock of starlings had gathered by one particularly large mound of decaying kelp, their beaks rapidly probing for fly larvae and other titbits thriving within its rotting embrace. We probably do not generally regard starlings as shore inhabitants, but they are resourceful birds and will often forage along beaches, seeking out masses of storm-tossed seaweed along the strandline. In amongst the starlings, rock pipits and pied wagtails also took advantage of the ephemeral riches of decaying seaweed, fluttering in short but determined flights to snap up tiny creatures attracted by the warmth of decomposition. Rock pipits are robust, grey-plumaged little songbirds, which as the name suggests, are specialists of rocky shores, taking advantage of the abundance of insect life, sandhoppers and other tiny creatures found in such places.

A strange object caught my eye by the strandline. It turned out to be the carapace of a masked crab, an animal that is rarely seen alive because they spend most of their time hiding in burrows in the sand below the waves. In a clever adaptation, the crab uses its two long antennae to form a breathing tube to deliver oxygenated water to its lair.

It was low tide and the lure of the sea edge soon drew me back down the beach, where I started to potter around some pools scattered across a rock shelf that bordered the sand. I turned a few rocks but the strength of the wind quickly froze my fingers, so I abandoned the search for pool creatures and instead walked slowly along the natural rock platform, scanning around my feet all the time. Encrusted on some rocks were the white scribble-like ridges made by keel worms; calcareous protective tube-like casings, which are a familiar feature of rocky shores. Their casts are incredibly hard and a bane for mariners as they can foul propellers and hulls.

A small group of wigeon ducks congregated in a little rocky channel, the lovely pinkish blush on the breasts of the drakes shining out across the wind-rippled rock pools. A cluster of eiders had gathered in a sheltered patch of sea between the shore and a shallow rocky reef, the drakes throwing back their heads as they courted the females. It may have only been February, but already thoughts of the breeding season ahead were uppermost in the thoughts of these handsome ducks.

Several carrion crows methodically picked their way over the rocks, turning over fronds of bladder wrack to search for creatures like crabs hiding beneath. As is the case with starlings, crows are intelligent birds and will frequently visit shorelines to forage.

Then, a shining glimmer from a patch of sand – it was the semi-buried shell of a bivalve mollusc and quite like any other on the shore. I prised it free from the clawing grip of the wet sand and cradled it in my hand. It was the half-shell of an ocean quahog, sometimes also known as the Icelandic cyprine. It had not long perished and the shell still gleamed bright, similar in colouration to a mussel, with a vibrant, glistening navy glint that almost bordered on black. It was a large clam-shaped shell – about 100 mm across at the widest point – and patterned with a series of paler concentric rings.

Ocean quahogs are among the longest-lived creatures known. One individual discovered by Icelandic researchers was found to be over 500 years old. As the animal grows, rings are laid down in the shell much in the same way as inside a tree trunk. The growth rings are at wider increments when conditions are more favourable and narrower when less so. By analysing these growth rings, scientists can delve into the past and determine changes in the marine environment that occurred over previous centuries. The ocean quahog in my hand was like an environmental history book that chronicled natural events in our seas over the past few centuries.

The ocean quahog is found on sandy and muddy sediments below 10 m depth and occurs all around Scotland, although most frequently in the northern North Sea. Sadly, it is thought this intriguing animal may be in decline, and one reason behind the establishment of the Firth of Forth Banks Complex Marine Protected Area, which covers a large area of undersea shelf banks and mounds stretching from the sea off Angus in the north down to Berwickshire in the south. The area is home to an array of other ecologically important and vulnerable creatures, including sandeels, brittle stars and soft corals, as well forming an important spawning ground for plaice.

I gently placed the ocean quahog shell back onto the patch of sand, my mind swirling with excitement about this natural antiquarian treasure. Taking renewed interest in the mollusc shells scattered around my feet, I ventured back to the wider expanse of sandy beach nearby. There was a broad mix of shells, which I began to collect, popping each shell into my jacket pocket. After a while, I laid each shell down onto the sand and examined my bounty. It was a rich harvest, which included a razorshell, queen scallop, horse mussel, prickly cockle, otter shell and several tellins.

Some of these molluscs, including the prickly cockle and otter shell, are mysterious denizens of our inshore waters living beneath the sand and mud and seldom seen in their living form. These shellfish feed by siphoning and filtering water to glean microscopic plankton. Filter feeding can be a hazardous business and the fleshy siphons that protrude above the sediment are often nipped-off by flatfish like flounders and dabs. Happily, the cropped siphons can regenerate, although this takes time, during which period the shellfish must lose vigour by being unable to feed properly.

One of the biggest threats facing inshore shellfish are storms. In shallow seas, the surging forces caused by tumultuous gales are immense and scour shellfish from their shelters in the soft substrate, causing large-scale mortalities.

Farther along the beach, the silvery-grey half-shell of an oyster glinted from the sand. Formerly abundant around Scottish coasts, a combination of pressure from harvesting and pollution led to the decline of the Firth of Forth oyster fishery, which ceased by 1920; by 1957, the species was believed to be extinct in the area. A similar pattern of sharp decline occurred in many other parts of Britain. Judging by the worn and heavily-eroded appearance of the shell, it seemed most likely this was a relic from the past when oysters were formerly abundant. A pity, perhaps, that my discovery wasn't related to a natural population resurgence in the Forth. However, an innovative and recently-launched initiative – Restoration Forth – intends to reinvigorate oyster populations in the area as part of its action plan, which will complement another scheme already established in the Dornoch Firth further north. It seems these intriguing molluscs might once more become a familiar part of our marine environment.

It transpires that the offshore sands in this part of the Forth protect other natural treasures from the past. The entry for Largo Bay from the *Ordnance Gazetteer Scotland* published in 1882 states:

> The bottom of the bay is mostly sandy, and forms excellent ground for line fishing. All along the coast extensive salmon fishings are carried on by fixed nets. Towards the east, beneath the sands are traces of submerged forest.

I stopped for a while to breathe in the invigorating sea air and contemplated the sands of Largo Bay as a natural repository for both past and present – remnants of ancient forest and antiquarian oyster shells, along with the vibrant life pulse of razorshells, cockles and a plethora of other creatures. The bay encapsulates what has been and where we are now, and with many species now in decline, perhaps also a glimpse into the future.

As I headed farther along the beach towards the rocky headland known as Ruddons Point, a swirling flock of ringed plovers wheeled past me before

Ringed Plover

alighting on the sand. They are energetic little waders, constantly on the move and patterned with distinctive black markings on the head and face, along with a most prominent white forehead.

Ringed plovers like to nest on sandy beaches which, unfortunately, are the very places that people love to roam with their dogs in spring and summer. The inevitable disturbance means that many nests fail resulting in ringed plover numbers becoming much diminished in recent times; another example of how our precious wildlife struggles to survive in an increasingly crowded world.

Chapter 28

WHY SIZE MATTERS & DEAD-MAN'S FINGERS

March 2023, North Ayrshire

Safety is paramount when snorkelling and a dilemma unfolded as I stood on a rocky promontory by Portencross Pier. It was a picturesque spot overlooking the Firth of Clyde towards the islands of Little Cumbrae and Arran – but the wind was picking up and the sea getting choppy.

I had spent the previous few days poring over maps for the next stage of my British travel journey – and during that time had developed a hankering to snorkel by a pier because such places provide shelter for an abundance of marine life. I had initially considered potential sites on Loch Long farther to the north but after much consideration, decided that Portencross Pier in North Ayrshire was a better option. The pier is an abandoned structure that stretches out a short distance from the shore, yet its steel piles are mounted in deep water and provide the ideal place for shellfish and other sea creatures to gain tenure.

Unfortunately, my plan was unravelling. I had chosen to snorkel at an extreme low spring tide, which would make it easier to dive down and witness creatures that would normally be hard to reach in deeper water. Low tide, however, was still a couple of hours away and while the surge in the sea was currently manageable, the weather forecast indicated a gale was brewing and if I delayed my entry into the water for much longer, snorkelling would become dangerous.

With time of the essence, I opted to forego the advantages brought by waiting for the tide to reach its lowest ebb and quickly donned my wet suit and slipped into the water, with a surge of sparkling bubbles swirling around my facemask. The visibility was reasonable – about 4 m – and I flicked my flippers until I reached the first of the steel piles that supported the T-shaped pier end.

Mussels and barnacles clung tenaciously to the upper parts of the stanchions. They are truly resilient creatures, able to withstand the rigours of storms, fierce currents and crashing waves without becoming dislodged from their holdfasts. On first impression, barnacles could easily be mistaken for molluscs, but curiously they are crustaceans and relatives of crabs, lobsters and prawns. Indeed, their planktonic larvae resemble those of crabs. The free-swimming larvae moult several times before sinking to a rock or other structure where they are attracted by the presence of other barnacles. Once settled, they cement themselves to the substrate using their antennae. The newly-rested barnacles moult once more, creating a final body structure of chalky fused plates, with a hatch-door opening at the top.

Millions of barnacles can occur along a kilometre of typical rocky shore and they are one of the most ubiquitous animals found on our coasts. When feeding, a barnacle opens the central plates on the top of its volcano-shaped shell and uses its modified legs ('cirri') to repeatedly claw at the water like a grasping hand reaching out for tiny floating organisms.

Apart from their larval stage, barnacles are stationary creatures, which makes breeding potentially problematic. Barnacles are hermaphrodites – having both male and female gonads – but to ensure genetic diversity by reaching out to cross-fertilise with other individuals, the animals have developed an incredibly long penis, which relative to body size, is thought to be the largest penis in the animal kingdom. In many barnacle species, when the eggs of an individual begin to develop, it turns into a functioning female that releases chemicals in the water. This alerts the neighbours, which become functioning males that unfurl their penises to search some distance from their resting spots to seek the right opening to fertilise the eggs.

The pioneering evolutionary biologist, Charles Darwin, was fascinated by barnacles and spent much of his time engaged in their research. He wrote:

> The males are attached at a considerable distance from the orifice of the sack of the female, into which the spermatozoa have to be conveyed; and to effect this, the prosciformed penis is wonderfully devel-oped...when fully extended, it must equal between eight and nine times the entire length of the animal!

While the barnacles and mussels on the upper pier supports were fascinating, my main interest lay in the deeper water below, and as my body rode the undulating waves, I peered down into the murky green depths, my eyes following the line of one of the pier supports. Just within the range of visibility, an orange glimmer shone out, and farther below on an adjacent stanchion there was a cluster of white. I took three deep breaths and dived under. The support was deeply encrusted with a myriad of algae and shells. On reaching the orange-glowed lifeform that had initially caught my attention, I steadied myself by holding onto the rough-crusted pier support. Before me lay the most exquisite creation, a cluster of orange-tinged fleshy lobes. Surrounding each lobe was a soft, opaque furred fuzz that on closer inspection was comprised of miniscule stalks tipped with white.

This was a soft coral known as dead-man's fingers, so called because it is said to resemble the swollen, decomposing hand of a dead person. Each 'finger' consists of a colony of tiny organisms, called polyps, set upon a shared gelatinous skeleton to form a greater whole. It is these polyps that create the furry appearance as they stand proud from the soft supporting body. Each polyp has a mouth surrounded by tiny tentacles which trap tiny food items in the water column. I imagine the name 'dead-man's fingers' is derived from times past when people searching for survivors from shipwrecks became overwhelmed by the stress of the occasion, sending their minds spinning into overdrive and suspecting the worst. Morbidly, the furred, translucent outer body resembles mould covering decomposing fingers.

I lingered under the water longer than intended and with lungs bursting rose back towards the surface at great speed, spurting water out of the snorkel on surfacing. In my younger days such a dive would have been executed with consummate ease, but now I was gasping and it took several moments to regain my composure and breathing. Once I had done so, I dived under again to investigate the white cluster that lay even deeper. This turned out to be a white form of dead-man's fingers, for it is a soft coral that exhibits considerable colour variation.

I surfaced once more and lay face down, spread-eagled on the water surface, my body heaving up and down on the increasing swell. The rising sea was giving cause for concern and there was a pressing need to exit the water, but before doing so, the temptation proved irresistible to snorkel under the pier while remaining on the surface. Here, on several of the pier supports lay a bewitching cornucopia of colour comprising large colonies of plumose anemones. Their beauty and form were breathtaking, elegant orange-brown anemones featuring long, slender tubular body columns with flickering tentacles that brimmed out over their tops like large, intricately-frilled umbrellas. As a biological comparison, these anemones were single polyps, compared to the integrated polyp colonies that form dead-man's fingers.

I endeavoured to take some photographs but the swirling water made it challenging to focus the camera and there was the danger that the sea surge would result in my head crashing into one of the barnacle-encrusted horizontal upper pier supports just above me. I slipped under the water to avoid such a mishap and surfaced a short distance from the pier in open water and swam quickly back to the rocky shore. On pulling myself out onto a flat rock shelf, I barely noticed the cold such was my excitement at glimpsing the anemones and dead-man's fingers. The sea was churning around the pier supports with increasing intensity and I breathed a sigh of relief at the decision to hastily abandon the snorkel.

Red-breasted Merganser

I packed my flippers, mask and weight belt into a small rucksack and hoisted it onto my back before carefully threading my way over the rocks as the wind whistled around with rising vigour. Out at sea, a small group of red-breasted mergansers bobbed in the white-flecked water and a rock pipit flitted up onto a nearby rock that was coated in a glistening layer of yellow lichen. Down by my feet on a grassy margin, the yellow spangled flowers of lesser celandine bloomed – my first sighting of the year of these brassy golden beauties.

I glanced round one last time at the pier and visualised the underwater garden of incredible colour and diversity that lay below the swelling sea. This was a place where beauty and danger were wrapped intimately as one and a stark reminder of the overwhelming power of nature.

Chapter 29

BEAVERS, BURRS & BEECHES

March 2023, Perthshire and Angus

There were plenty signs of beaver activity as I ambled along the bankside of the River Earn near Crieff in Perthshire. Some small birches had been felled and parts of the bark of other trees had been stripped. One tree really caught my eye because it looked as if there were nodules of fungus growing close to where a beaver had been gnawing.

I brushed my fingers across the spherical golf-ball sized growths. They were hard and an integral part of the tree itself. Rather than fungi, these were burrs – rounded growths that are often a reaction to stress, such as injury or damage, insect attack, or bacterial or fungal infection. Sometimes burrs can become very large, but these were small and rounded.

Burrs are in effect a protection mechanism, forming over or near an area of trauma to prevent any further damage. They do not harm the tree and are part of nature's tapestry of intricate responses to the daily challenges of life. In woodwork, large burrs can be much sought after because of the unique swirling patterns they instil in the grain of the wood.

Beavers occur in good numbers on the River Earn, which was the Scottish river where they first mysteriously appeared around the year 2000, most likely as escapees from an animal collection. Since then, they have spread widely throughout the Tay river catchment and are now colonising some of the rivers that drain into the Firth of Forth. Beavers are controversial and some farmers and landowners are concerned by their presence because they fell trees and their dams can cause flooding by blocking drainage ditches. They may also damage crops. As such, it is permissible in Scotland to cull beaver populations under licence in areas where they are deemed to be causing problems.

Whilst there is legitimacy to such concerns and eking a living from the land is often a thankless task that requires hard toil, surely it is not beyond the wit of humankind in the twenty-first century to live with nature, rather than constantly oppose and control it. Beavers have been swimming in our rivers, lochs and lakes since the dawn of time until they were hunted into extinction around the sixteenth century. Beavers belong here, they are part of our landscape, and research has shown that their presence delivers tangible environmental benefits, including increased biodiversity. The ponds created by beaver dams brim with invertebrates, amphibians and water plants, and their dams slow the flow of water, preventing flooding farther downstream during periods of heavy rain. Felled trees are often coppiced rather than killed, and the resultant sun-dappled clearings created abound with wildflowers and insects.

Beaver & Birch Trees

Various mitigation measures can be taken to cushion any deleterious impact of beavers on agricultural land, and in worst case scenarios, beavers should be translocated to other sites rather than culled. Thankfully, translocations are now recognised as a viable and sensible option, which has the additional benefit of aiding their spread to other parts of the country, including, in recent times, Loch Lomond, and with the considerable potential to act as a source to repopulate areas of England and Wales.

I moved farther along the riverbank and stopped to watch a pair of buzzards soar high above the river on wide-held wings. This pair were thinking about breeding and it was beguiling to watch them displaying to one another in the sky, their haunting mewing calls carrying far in the wind as they circled on the updrafts.

Then, my attention was caught by a red glimmer by the path side, shining with the intensity of a glowing ember. I crouched down to examine this ruby gem, which turned out to be a scarlet elfcup. I couldn't recall the last time I had encountered this scarce fungus, but it was certainly a while ago – they are delicate in their shape and form. They are most often found in late winter and early spring, and as the name suggests, the cap is cup-shaped. Also known as 'fairies baths', folklore has it that wood elves and fairies drank morning dew from scarlet elfcups.

Nearby, tiers of turkey-tail fungus clung to a branch. This is a distinctive species which should have been past its best by now, but this cluster was an exception and still exhibited vibrancy.

A cock chaffinch fluttered up into a birch ahead of me. He remained silent, but soon would be heard uttering his spring song. It is a simple song, lacking the depth and variation found in other birds. On a visit to British shores, John Burroughs, the renowned late nineteenth- and early twentieth-century American naturalist, was amazed at the number of chaffinches he heard: 'I have never heard a song that began so liltingly end with such a quick, abrupt emphasis'.

Buzzard Over The River Earn At Kinkell Bridge

On the far bank of the Earn, a blackbird sang his rich and deep melody that drifted across the river like a welcoming herald to spring; sweet and pure, and encapsulating perfectly the season of new life. The blackbird reminded me of the dawn chorus I had listened to in woodland in nearby Clackmannanshire only the day before. It was early morning and still dark, the sun having another hour or so until it breached the horizon. Yet, nature was stirring. A fluty pair of notes from a song thrush piped-up, followed by another couplet of musical brilliance, so pure and clear it drifted across the dark air like a haunting lament.

Farther away, another song thrush lilted his spring song as if in a musical competition. The contemporary poet, Thistle Wargul, wrote charmingly of the song thrush:

> So sweetly you sing little song thrush
> Though speckled brown only you are
> With a delicate voice like a piccolo
> Skylark, blackbird and robin
> Are jealous you sound so nice.

Mesmerised by the piccolo dawn music, I closed my eyes and let its ethereal beauty ripple across my soul. *How could these delicate birds produce a song of such incredible depth and perfect pitch quality?* Whenever I dwell upon nature, there are many questions and so few answers. I have long since concluded that the 'why' is largely irrelevant, it is only the actuality that matters.

The song thrush has one of the longest singing periods of any bird – sometimes beginning in late December and not finishing until the end of August, a marathon songster that brings glorious enchantment to the world.

I adore rivers and my visit to the River Earn inspired me later that week to travel farther northeast to explore the River North Esk near the village of Edzell, which lies on the border between Angus and Aberdeenshire. By the roadside, a blue door set in a heavy stone wall provided access to a walk along the North Esk that leads to a spectacular riverside section known as the 'Rocks of Solitude'. The blue door was an enticement, a beckoning call to open and explore as if acting as an entrance to a different world. I gently pushed the door open, leaving behind the road and became immersed in the turbulent splendour of the river gorge.

On peering down a steep slope towards the gushing river, the deep, coppery hue of the water was most striking, like swirling amber whisky that had been drawn from the depths of the earth. A dipper whirred upriver, spiralling over a rock shelf before disappearing.

Beech trees towered above the main path, the pale smooth bark of their trunks catching the soft luminescence of the afternoon sun. Gilbert White, the pioneering eighteenth-century nature diarist, described the beech as 'the most lovely of all forest trees, whether we consider its smooth rind or bark, its glossy foliage, or graceful pendulous boughs'.

Naturalist, Richard Mabey, in his *Flora Britannica* noted that the beech has something of a feminine image – an example of elegance that acted as a foil to the rugged masculinity of the oak. As I ran my hand down the smooth bark of one beech, I understood what he meant, for the beech is polished perfection, genteel yet with an inner strength.

The roots of beech spread laterally just below the soil surface, rendering the trees vulnerable to gales, and several along the path had tumbled from recent storms. Their demise is part and parcel of nature, the rotting wood providing a place for fungi and invertebrates to thrive, and the sun-cascaded openings created in the high canopy benefiting plants on the woodland floor.

A treecreeper spiralled its way up the trunk of a beech ahead of me, its long, curved bill probing every nook and cranny for small invertebrates. It climbed halfway up, and then fluttered down to the base of an adjacent tree to start the process all over again. The smooth bark of beeches must make them less productive places to forage compared with gnarled oaks and their abundance of insect-sheltering crevices. Yet, this treecreeper seemed content with its pickings, especially in areas where moss had accumulated.

I wandered down a small side path that led to a broad rock shelf above a narrow channel hewn in the rock by the river. Here lay a most spectacular chasm of rocky waterfalls and deep coppery-coloured pools that provided the perfect encapsulation of the raw power of nature: a myriad of stark rock, dizzying heights and churning water.

On my return journey, a party of long-tailed tits bounded through the trees, restless birds that are forever on the move. Soon I reached the blue door once more, pulled it open and departed from the wild allure of the tumble-watered gorge and slipped back into the hectic world of humanity.

Chapter 30

GLEN DYE MEMORIES

April 2023, Aberdeenshire

Glen Dye is an old stomping ground of mine that holds strong in my heart. On these magical moors, I have glimpsed golden eagles and hen harriers, mountain hares and black grouse, and watched a pair of tumbling merlins chase one another across the sky.

Golden Eagle & Hen Harrier

Situated to the south of Banchory on Deeside, this vast sweep of hill, moor, woodland and gushing burns has helped shape my very being. For a period of ten years or so from the mid-1980s onwards, I visited the area frequently, exploring every corner of the hills and becoming completely addicted to its wild charms. Glen Dye even functioned as a comfort blanket when I needed solace to cry over matters of love, such was its spiritual hold.

A change in employment then took me away from the northeast of Scotland, and ever since I have been reluctant to return to the glen. Paradoxically, this was because my adoration for the place was so overwhelming, there was an innate fear that a revisit would disappoint and fail to meet expectations. Fortunately, for my British wildlife journey, I pushed aside such irrationality and mustered the courage to explore its wild expanses once more.

The approach by road from the south, across the Highland Boundary Fault, provides a dramatic introduction to the glen's enticing embrace. Buoyed by a wave of euphoria, I drove over the high top of the Cairn o' Mount gateway, unveiling beyond an ochre-burnished vista of rolling hills and moor, backdropped by the distinctive granite tor of Clachnaben.

Inevitably, memories flooded back in a rush that was impossible to quell. In a strange and contradictory way, the allure of Glen Dye revolved around its normality and lack of grandeur. These are not dramatic and imposing hills and mountains, such as found in the Cairngorms or northwest Highlands. Instead, this was a landscape of low rounded tops; mild and meek in comparison to much else that Scotland has to offer. It is this unremarkable aspect I find most appealing – an anonymous place that holds wild secrets waiting to be discovered. Curiously, I am drawn in much the same way to people – shying away from those with outgoing personalities and attracted more to those with a quieter demeanour. Invariably, when one delves beneath the initial deceptive cloak of modesty, a rich tapestry of inner depth is revealed.

The domed top of Meluncart which looms over the southern flank of Glen Dye is a case in point. It is an unremarkable little hill, yet one where many years ago I enjoyed a spellbinding winter wildlife spectacle that is still engrained upon my memory to this day. The ground was snow free and a strong frigid wind blew under a weak and watery sun. Against the bleakness of the peat hags, I was astonished to encounter a multitude of mountain hares, their white-furred coats contrasting starkly against the dark peat and heather. They were all moving slowly just below the summit in a clockwise direction. I lost count of the number of animals after reaching 50 and still they came as if drawn by an invisible force. I have never since witnessed so many mountain hares together at the same time and can only surmise that they were sheltering in the lee of the hill from the bitter wind.

Mountain Hares, Clachnaben

As the memory flashbacks continued to unfurl, I parked the car by a forest track and set out on a circuit that would take me around the north side of the tops of Mount Shade and Clachnaben, and on towards the flat, heathery expanse of Airy Muir at an altitude of around 450 m, before descending into Glen Dye via the Hill of Edendocher. As I worked my way up through the forest, my mind still in a dreamy drift, a woodcock exploded from under my feet and with the accuracy of a guided missile flew unerringly through the wire-mesh gap of a deer fence, twisting and turning as it went. Woodcocks have large, penetrating eyes, and I imagine its superb vision aided its pinpoint trajectory.

The woodcock stirred recollections of when I used to watch these mystical birds engage in their 'roding' display flights at dusk above a forest clearing near the Water of Dye, the small river that runs down the glen. These gloaming moments were truly special, the light slowly fading and the wind dropping to create an air of quiet serenity that soothed the soul. Then, a roding woodcock would appear – a male heading towards me, skimming low over the treetops on flickering owl-like wings and uttering strange croaks and intermittent hissy chirps. Over my head he would fly, disappearing behind a high bank of trees. All would be quiet again, but the woodcock had a favoured territorial circuit he patrolled, so I would wait in excited anticipation. Sure enough, a short while later he would sweep back into view, uttering his croaks and chirps, and skidding across the diminishing sky like a phantom of the dusk.

In the past, the woodcock was known as the 'moon bird' because it was thought that they went to the moon in autumn as reflected by the early eighteenth-century poet, John Gay:

> He sung where woodcocks in the summer feed
> And in what climates they renew their breed
> Some think to northern coasts their flight they tend
> Or, to the moon in midnight hours ascend.

Interestingly, at the time of the poem, most woodcocks possibly did go elsewhere in Europe to 'renew their breed', with deforestation in previous centuries having diminished suitable woodland nesting habitat for them in much of Britain.

The first section of the forest walk was comprised of towering Scots pines under which flourished a rich understorey of heather and blaeberry, which bore great similarity to the true ancient remnants of Caledonian wildwood that still exist in nearby Glen Tanar on Deeside and in the Cairngorms and Strathspey beyond. Many moons ago, I once glimpsed a cock capercaillie in this very same wood. Tragically, numbers of these large woodland grouse have plummeted since and they now have a precarious foothold in only a few parts of Scotland.

I broke out of the forest and skirted around the imposing granite tor of Clachnaben and out onto open moorland. The name of this distinctive hill derives from 'Clach na Beinne', or 'the stone of the hill'. Adam Watson, the renowned Scottish ecologist who knew these hills intimately, described the rocky outcrop as looking like a 'gigantic wart'. To the north, the distinctive top of Bennachie etched the horizon. The two tops and their proximity to the coast were a familiar landmark to fishermen, giving rise to the old couplet: *'Clachnaben and Bennachie, Are twa landmarks frae the sea'.*

Farther to the west, the domed top of Mount Battock hove into view. Adam Watson in his book, *The Cairngorms*, wrote that Mount Battock was notable as being the furthest east hill in Scotland where ptarmigan nest. I am not sure if they still do so – I have climbed the hill several times but never glimpsed ptarmigan on the summit.

Above me, a skylark spiralled up into the air, raining forth his melodic song. Shakespeare described the skylark as 'the herald of the morn' and as this one soared ever higher, his song was indeed an inspiring beckoning to the joys of a new day. After hanging in the air for a while, he made a slow descent and disappeared among a thick flush of heather.

Meadow pipits fluttered up into the air before me, excited by the onset of spring and eagerly seeking mates. Their trilling song flights may not be as dramatic as those of the skylark, but they are still wonderful to watch as they ascend and float down on parachute wings.

A green-fringed sphagnum pool brought me to a halt and I peered into its peaty depths in the hope of spotting palmate newts. None could be seen, but I knew from experience that these upland pools are ecologically important, offering important breeding places for amphibians and a wide range of aquatic invertebrates. Their upland nature means the water is cold and nutrient poor, and in many of these pools, especially in the high

Palmate Newt

Cairngorms, it often takes a couple of years for newt tadpoles to fully develop.

On my descent into Glen Dye, I stumbled upon another pool, which this time brimmed with life. Pondweed abounded, around which long strings of toad spawn had been carefully entwined. In among the weed, there was the flickering movement of a palmate newt. I scooped it out with cupped hands and admired the attractive orange tones along its spotted flanks, before gently placing the amphibian back into the water so that it could resume once more its quest to breed.

The route down into the glen took me to the stone-built Charr Bothy, a shelter for walkers which is maintained by the Mountain Bothies Association. On evening walks more than 30 years ago, I used to sit by the bothy and watch a colony of rabbits that lived around it and soon became engrossed by their activities. Rather than being simple animals, the rabbit has a complex social life where a strict hierarchy is maintained, with the dominant males siring the most offspring and the lead females having access to the best burrows. Such a pecking order was easy to discern amongst the Glen Dye rabbits, with the peaceful evening scene of small groups feeding on the short grass occasionally interrupted by short chases as a dominant animal tried to see off a lesser one.

If danger threatened, such as when I made a noise as I moved to return home, then the scatter of rabbits down into their burrows would sometimes be accompanied by a distinct thump of the back feet which acted as a warning signal. Another interesting feature of the Glen Dye rabbits was that a few of them were black, a genetic aberration probably aided by the relative isolation of the colony.

As I sat on a rock by the bothy engaged in such reflections, I speculated whether the rabbits were still there. I scanned the ground but could not detect their signs, and given the small size and remoteness of the colony, deduced that they were probably now extinct, having fallen victim to disease or a prolonged frosty winter.

On my return along the glen, I scoured the tracksides for adders basking in the sun. Whilst there was no sign of snakes, I was rewarded with the sight of several green tiger beetles, which scuttled across the path like emerald jewels, their vibrant bodies glistening in the sun.

Despite their attractive appearance, green tiger beetles are ferocious mini predators that feed upon small spiders and insects. They have an impressive turn of speed and are one of Britain's fastest insects.

As I followed the course of the Water of Dye towards my end destination, my mind was awash with countless other memories of this wild and lonely place, which were so overwhelming I found it nigh-on impossible to concentrate upon the nature around me. But I didn't really care, for I was back where I belonged and that was all that mattered.

Green Tiger Beetle

Chapter 31

STUNNING NUDIBRANCHS, A BURROWING RAZORSHELL & SOARING SEA EAGLES

April 2023, Wester Ross and Sutherland

It was the strangest phenomenon – white spirals on the sandy bottom of a sea loch in the northwest Highlands that resembled loosely-coiled strips of gauze. Such was their unusual appearance, I wondered whether this might be a form of plastic pollution, but they were loosely anchored to the seabed in a manner that suggested this was some natural creation.

Intrigued, I took three deep breaths and dived down to investigate further. I gently touched one with my forefinger and the white spiral form was soft and yielding, and slightly gelatinous. These bizarre objects were undoubtedly a part of nature. I surfaced and blew water out my snorkel tube, and as I lay on the surface to regain breath, I racked my brains as to what these unusual objects were. The pondering was quickly interrupted by a faint scarlet glimmering on the sea floor, so I dived down once more to be rewarded by a close encounter with one of the most exquisite creatures imaginable. It was a nudibranch, or sea slug, which was about 100 mm long with intricate red patterning set upon an oval, flattened body. On the upper surface were paler, fleshy tubercles. Adorning the top of the head was a pair of horned projections known as rhinophores, which are sensory organs that detect chemicals in the water and aid in finding food, mates and avoiding predators.

Elated by the discovery, I surfaced again and slowly swam along the surface scanning the seabed below. Once my eyes had become accustomed to their shape and form, more nudibranchs appeared, some of which had paired up with other ones. It was apparent the animals had moved inshore to breed and the weird white spiral objects were their egg masses. I had never witnessed this species before and, as far as I am aware, it has no common English name, instead it is known by its scientific nomenclature, *Pleurobranchus membranaceus*.

Nudibranchs are fascinating creatures and colourful marvels of nature; molluscs that lack a protective shell. To overcome the lack of hard external protection against predators, nudibranchs employ noxious chemical defence mechanisms to discourage attack, and the bright colouration of the animals acts as a warning signal for predators to keep their distance, much in the same manner as the vibrant yellow and black striped patterning of a wasp. Some nudibranchs even requisition stinging venomous cells from jellyfish and anemones and use them as armament for their own defence.

I was snorkelling at Ardmair Bay a few kilometres north of Ullapool, which is an offshoot of Loch Broom in Wester Ross. It is an excellent site for snorkelling, and the size and scope of the bay, combined with the protection offered by Isle Martin, which lies just offshore, makes it a safe and sheltered place to explore its rich marine life.

Using a caravan as my base over the course of a week, I snorkelled daily and was continually enthralled by exciting wildlife discoveries that unveiled before my eyes at a bewildering rate, including huge spiny starfish, their splayed arms easily covering the diameter of a dinner plate. Also present were smaller common starfish and sand stars, the latter is a creature I do not often encounter when snorkelling. Sand stars have chunkier bodies than starfish, with shorter arms.

On one occasion, as I floated over a shallow section of mixed seabed comprising sand, seaweed and rocks, a razorshell swam just below me, moving in erratic jerks before floating down and coming to rest on the seabed. Razorshells spend most of their time buried under sand, with just a siphon protruding above the sediment to filter food. I could not recall ever having seen a living razorshell before and it never occurred to me they could swim. As I peered down at the sleek elongated shell lying horizontally on the seabed, the animal suddenly flipped up into the vertical position and used its muscular foot to quickly pull itself completely under the sand. It was one of the most remarkable wildlife sights I ever witnessed, a mollusc moving with speed and dexterity, and with an all-encompassing awareness of its surroundings.

Not long after, I noticed a frond of kelp waving frenetically, and closer inspection revealed a large whelk that had turned its spiral shell over onto its back as it sought prey hiding on the underside of the broad blade of seaweed. Whelks are carnivorous, feeding on worms, crustaceans, mussels and other molluscs. The whelk seemed to sense my body hovering above and quickly turned back over to its normal upright position to provide protection to its vulnerable underparts. Again, this was a remarkable display of agile shellfish behaviour. I wondered how the whelk had detected my presence in the first instance. Whelks have simple eyes that can probably only discern varying light intensities, so perhaps the shade of my body had alerted it, or more likely, chemoreceptors in its sensory tentacles had sniffed me out.

While the underwater glories of Ardmair Bay were absorbing, I also spent much time tramping the nearby hills and exploring other parts of this diverse and beautiful part of northwest Scotland. One remarkable sight was a large tumbling burn, which appeared miraculously from solid rock as if spirited into existence by natural wizardry. This was a natural spring near the Inchnadamph 'Bone Caves' in Assynt, Sutherland, where a subterranean stream emerges from the ground, bubbling up through a deep bed of gravel that is a feature of the limestone geology of the area. It was a spontaneous creation that made the mind spin in wonderment at the forces which had forged the ground beneath me.

The nearby caves set in an elevated position on the steep-sided slope of a glen are an open door to our prehistoric past where brown bear and reindeer bones were unearthed by geologists in the late 1880s. More recent digs have revealed the remains of other animals that once roamed Britain, including Arctic fox, lemming, lynx, wolf and wild horse. A fragment of a polar bear's skull, which is estimated to be over 20,000 years old, was even discovered in one cave. Some of the bones may have been washed into the caves by melting glaciers, but the caves were also used as a shelter by animals, and later, by people.

Liverworts and small ferns clung tenaciously to the cave wall entrances. These primitive plants thrive in dark, damp environments. Liverworts are easily overlooked, but they are intriguing, small flowerless plants with leaf-like lobes, which appear like a lobed liver, hence the name. Liverworts produce spores to reproduce instead of flowers and seeds and they provide important microhabitats for tiny creatures.

On another day, a hike over moorland took me to remote Slaggan Bay, a beautiful sweep of sand at the mouth of Loch Ewe. It is a place I return to regularly, and each visit is always tinged with a degree of emotion, for during the Second World War my father had, on occasion, departed Loch Ewe as a young Royal Navy officer heading out on the Arctic Convoys to Murmansk in northern Russia – a voyage Winston Churchill dubbed 'the worst journey in the world'.

Out in the water of Slaggan Bay, a lone great northern diver bobbed in the calm sea, frequently roll-diving under in its quest for fish. This diver – which is known as the common loon in North America – would shortly be heading to its Icelandic breeding grounds. Nearby, a pair of smaller black-throated divers floated, resplendent with their dark shield-shaped throats and half-collars streaked with black and white. The pair worked as a team when fishing, diving under in unison to cover as broad an extent of seabed as possible. I imagine that if one diver disturbed a fish, there was every chance the prey would flee straight into the path of its compatriot. Closer inshore, a trio of red-breasted mergansers – a male and two females – fished in the same manner, diving under as a group in the hope of flushing out flounders and dabs lying buried in the sand.

There is a steep sandy slope at the back of the beach, and on a visit to Slaggan Bay the previous August, I was thrilled by the sight of buzzing hordes of girdled colletes bees, which are a type of mining bee. These small striped bees were engaged in a mating frenzy, with little clusters of the insects squirming over one another on the ground, creating little balls of tumbling life that clung desperately to one another. This was a place where each season delivers new and different wildlife spectacles.

Another venture took me on a hill circuit from Ullapool up to the small top of Maol Chalaisgeig before dropping down to Loch Achall and then back to the start point. Close to Loch Achall, a white-tailed eagle soared above a ridge, its broad wings outspread as if seeking every ounce of updraft for lift. It gained more height before half-closing its wings and diving down over the far side of a nearby hill. White-tailed eagles, or sea eagles as they are also known, are one of Scotland's conservation success stories after having been persecuted to extinction by the start of the twentieth century. A reintroduction scheme began on the Isle of Rum

White-tailed Eagle (Sea Eagle) Fishing

in 1974 and in 1985 the first wild chick from the reintroduced population hatched on Mull. Now, there are approaching 200 breeding pairs.

White-tailed Eagle (Sea Eagle)

Like the beaver, such introductions can prove controversial, and in the case of white-tailed eagles there are concerns among farmers over lambs being taken. However, as with the beaver, white-tailed eagles are native and an integral part of the environment. They also bring economic benefits. A recent study commissioned by RSPB Scotland revealed that on the Isle of Mull, tourism inspired by these birds attracted between £4.9 and £8 million of spend annually, which supported up to 160 jobs.

Unusually for April in the northwest Highlands, the sun shone brightly for the whole week and the sea remained calm, and after each day in the hills, the lure of a late afternoon snorkel in Ardmair Bay proved irresistible. On the last day, I plunged into a sheltered corner of the bay for a final snorkel and ventured towards the same shallow area where I had previously spotted the dynamic movements of the razorshell and whelk. By a sandy margin close to a kelp bed, the long, sinuous tentacles of a tube anemone flickered. The anemone was housed in a calcareous tube mostly buried in the sediment, with only a centimetre of the uppermost section poking above the surface. The long tapering, brownish tentacles of the anemone spilled over the top of tube, seeking to trap miniscule food items floating past in the water.

Tube Anenome

A further search in the immediate vicinity revealed a couple of other tube anemones, which left me questioning how I had never spotted this cluster when I had explored the area before. It was possible that previously the anemones had their tentacles retracted, making them inconspicuous, but more likely my attention had been diverted elsewhere when I passed over them.

A short while later, a colourful disc of red and blue-grey glinted from the seabed. It was a dahlia anemone, another new discovery for me in the bay. Nearby, several more lay scattered on the coarse sandy sediment and were surrounded by thick flushes of shimmering seaweed. The anemones had a body base circumference of about 50 mm and the tentacles were short and brightly toned. It is the largest and most spectacular of our sea anemones that feeds on a variety of small invertebrates. As the tentacles curl over the prey, nematocysts – which are like tiny poisonous harpoons – discharge and paralyse their capture.

Dahlia anemones are well-named for they bear a strong resemblance to dahlia flowers, and as I drifted away from them and into a thick understorey of limey-green sea lettuces and other vibrant seaweeds, it felt like I was privy to the enchanting world of a secret underwater garden where colour shone in every direction and new nature surprises unfolded at every turn.

Chapter 32

JOURNEY'S END IN THE WILD BEAUTY OF DUNNET HEAD

April 2023, Caithness

The sea mist billowed around Dunnet Head in Caithness, shrouding the clifftops in a ghostly cloak, before momentarily receding to reveal scores of seabirds on their nesting ledges below. It was a heartrending moment, for I was at the culmination of my year-long wildlife journey which began at mainland Britain's southernmost edge, Lizard Point in Cornwall, and now was ending here at Dunnet Head, the most northern point.

It had been an eclectic and eye-opening journey, taking in England's green and pleasant land, exploring the wonderful wilds of Wales and ending in the stark beauty of Scotland's north coast. There were numerous highlights, and as a I rattled them off in my mind, the sheer diversity of life and variety of landscape found on this wind-blown island in the northeast Atlantic became searingly apparent.

I had been mesmerised by the rattling songs of Cetti's warblers in southern England and awed by choughs soaring above the Pembrokeshire cliffs. There had been bottlenose dolphins in Cardigan Bay and banded demoiselle damselflies in Norfolk, along with ospreys on Rutland Water and spoonbills in Lincolnshire. Northern England delivered encounters with barnacle geese and fascinating woodland fungi, while Scotland brought me close to the sanderlings of Largo Bay and mysterious ocean quahog molluscs that can live for hundreds of years. The island of Britain and its associated myriad of isles is incredibly rich in nature and there is much to celebrate. Equally, there is much to be seriously concerned about.

A recent study led by the Natural History Museum revealed that the UK is one of the world's most nature-depleted countries, with, on average, about half its biodiversity left – far below the global average of 75 per cent. The UK is in the bottom 10 per cent globally and last among the G7 group of nations – consisting of Canada, France, Germany, Italy, Japan, UK and USA.

There are polluted rivers, creeping urbanisation, overgrazing on our uplands, and loss of meadows and woodlands, and so many other environmental issues. Climate change is negatively impacting our seas and air pollution is hitting human health. The problems are immense and urgent action is needed to address them. With the UK being among the richest countries in the world, it is within the grasp of the UK government, industry and its wider populace to make the changes necessary to improve both its environment, and with it, the population's overall wellbeing. Nature is incredibly resilient and will thrive if given the chance to do so – but it must be given that opportunity.

On the positive side, nature and the wider environment has become a topic of great interest and passion for many, which means that the irrepressible force of 'people power' has the potential to drive the change that is needed. Yes, we need to farm to ensure there is food on our plates, and people need economic security, but all that can be achieved without detriment to nature if the correct measures and regimes are put in place. Without nature, we are nothing.

As these thoughts coursed through my head, my attention returned to the inspiring panorama of Dunnet Head. The sea mist, or haar as it is known in Scotland, tantalisingly ebbed and flowed, intermittently covering the cliff faces that bounded the Pentland Firth. In a strange coincidence, this was a mirror image of the end point for my previous book – A Scottish Wildlife Odyssey – which had culminated on the towering cliffs of Hermaness on Unst in Shetland, where thick mist had hung heavy in the air, obscuring the view yet simultaneously lifting the heart. When something is hidden, the mind stirs into action, picturing the unseen and conjuring visions that tell a thousand stories from past encounters with nature. My mind also tried to visualise the nearby red cliffs of Hoy on the Orkney Islands, which were concealed by the mist. James Miller in his book, Portrait of Caithness and Sutherland, described Dunnet Head as a 'great fist of heather and sandstone, in effect a moorland plateau with lochs crouching in folds in the ground and girt about with a red cliff wall'.

I sat on a grassy hummock by Dunnet Head for a while longer and watched the haar pull back farther out to sea, unveiling elegant kittiwakes swooping and swirling in the updrafts of briny air. Kittiwakes are such graceful gulls, perfectly proportioned and with a bewitching beauty.

A flock of guillemots flew low over the water in a goose-like V-formation, using their guile to fly in the most efficient manner possible. Nearby, a small group of gannets flew past, their wings digging powerfully into the air. I speculated which breeding colony they hailed from – possibilities included the archipelago of St Kilda to the west of the Outer Hebrides, the Isle of Noss in Shetland, or Troup Head in Aberdeenshire. Gannets wander far during the breeding season, which is useful for raising chicks as it enables parent birds to seek out the best fishing grounds over a broad area, ensuring a plentiful supply of food for hungry young mouths.

A pair of courting razorbills caught my eye on a grassy ledge by the clifftop. They preened one another and bobbed their heads up and down excitedly as they strengthened their pair bond. In a flash, the female crouched down and the male alighted upon her back to mate. The act was over in a moment, and he fluttered down beside her to nibble her neck once more with his razor-shaped bill. The next generation had been created, and with it, new life and new hope.

Razorbills

While guillemots opt to nest on impossibly small, vertical cliff ledges, razorbills prefer broader shelves on which to lay their eggs. Razorbills live mostly out at sea, only coming ashore to breed, which means they are poorly adapted for life on land, and finding walking difficult, they adopt an ungainly shuffle.

Fulmars also huddled in pairs on the ledges like besotted lovebirds. The name fulmar originates from the old Norse 'foul-gull' in reference to its habit of regurgitating its oily stomach contents as a noxious defence mechanism should one approach too close. Despite this, in the past fulmar vomit was held in great esteem by the inhabitants of St Kilda and was used as a treatment for a variety of ailments such as dental abscesses and rheumatism. The people of St Kilda relied upon nature for their existence, just as we all do today.

While these seabirds on the cliffs below brought joy to my heart, like much of our other wildlife, they too are exposed to an ever-increasing array of threats, most notably Bird Flu in recent times, which has affected some species especially badly, including great skuas. The razorbills, fulmars and kittiwakes at Dunnet Head also brought home to me the key element that makes Britain so special – the sea. Nowhere in the British Isles is far from the coast and it is the sea that warms our shores and drives the weather, creating a wonderfully rich environment.

By my side prospered a clump of thrift, the flowerheads yet to burst forth with their pink-frilled blooms. When I began my journey at Lizard Point over 900 km farther south at about the same time the previous year, thrift was already in flower, underlining the scope of geography and natural variation that lies at the heart of Britain.

Puffins had gathered on a steep grassy bank on one of the cliff faces below me, which was pockmarked with their nesting burrows. The haar tumbled back in again, concealing them under its wispy veil. While the puffins and other seabirds had vanished in the mist, their calls continued to drift across the air, so I closed my eyes and revelled in their addictive beauty. My journey may have finished, but the wild seabird cries will ring in my head forever, an evocative endorsement to the diverse nature found across this wonderful land and a warning call for the threats of the future.

Puffin

A SCOTTISH WILDLIFE ODYSSEY

In Search of Scotland's Wild Secrets

SHORTLISTED AUTHOR
Scotland's National Book Awards

Keith Broomfield

'Poetic, thoughtful, charming and informative.'

A Scottish River Wildlife Journey

KEITH BROOMFIELD

OTHER TITLES FROM
TIPPERMUIR BOOKS

Spanish Thermopylae (2009)

Battleground Perthshire (2009)

Perth: Street by Street (2012)

Born in Perthshire (2012)

In Spain with Orwell (2013)

Trust (2014)

Perth: As Others Saw Us (2014)

Love All (2015)

A Chocolate Soldier (2016)

The Early Photographers of Perthshire (2016)

Taking Detective Novels Seriously: The Collected Crime Reviews
    of Dorothy L Sayers (2017)

Walking with Ghosts (2017)

No Fair City: Dark Tales from Perth's Past (2017)

The Tale o the Wee Mowdie that wantit tae ken wha keeched on
    his heid (2017)

Hunters: Wee Stories from the Crescent: A Reminiscence of
    Perth's Hunter Crescent (2017)

A Little Book of Carol's (2018)

Flipstones (2018)

Perth: Scott's Fair City: The Fair Maid of Perth & Sir Walter Scott –
    A Celebration & Guided Tour (2018)

God, Hitler, and Lord Peter Wimsey: Selected Essays, Speeches and
    Articles by Dorothy L Sayers (2019)

Perth & Kinross: A Pocket Miscellany: A Companion for Visitors
    and Residents (2019)

The Piper of Tobruk: Pipe Major Robert Roy, MBE, DCM (2019)

The 'Gig Docter o Athole': Dr William Irvine & The Irvine Memorial
    Hospital (2019)

Afore the Highlands: The Jacobites in Perth, 1715–16 (2019)

'Where Sky and Summit Meet': Flight Over Perthshire – A History: Tales of Pilots, Airfields, Aeronautical Feats, & War (2019)

Diverted Traffic (2020)

Authentic Democracy: An Ethical Justification of Anarchism (2020)

'If Rivers Could Sing': A Scottish River Wildlife Journey. A Year in the Life of the River Devon as it flows through the Counties of Perthshire, Kinross-shire & Clackmannanshire (2020)

A Squatter o Bairnrhymes (2020)

In a Sma Room Songbook: From the Poems by William Soutar (2020)

The Nicht Afore Christmas: the much-loved yuletide tale in Scots (2020)

Ice Cold Blood (2021)

The Perth Riverside Nursery & Beyond: A Spirit of Enterprise and Improvement (2021)

Fatal Duty: The Scottish Police Force to 1952: Cop Killers, Killer Cops & More (2021)

The Shanter Legacy: The Search for the Grey Mare's Tail (2021)

'Dying to Live': The Story of Grant McIntyre, Covid's Sickest Patient (2021)

The Black Watch and the Great War (2021)

Beyond the Swelkie: A Collection of Poems & Writings to Mark the Centenary of George Mackay Brown (2021)

Sweet F.A. (2022)

A War of Two Halves (2022)

A Scottish Wildlife Odyssey (2022)

In the Shadow of Piper Alpha (2022)

Mind the Links: Golf Memories (2022)

Perthshire 101: A Poetic Gazetteer of the Big County (2022)

The Banes o the Turas: An Owersettin in Scots o the Poems bi Pino Mereu scrievit in Tribute tae Hamish Henderson (2022)

Walking the Antonine Wall (2022)

The Japan Lights (2023)

Fat Girl Best Friend (2023)

Guid Mornin! Guid Nicht! (Lawrence Schimel and Elīna Brasliņa, Scots translation by Matthew Mackie, 2023)

Madainn Mhath! Oidhche Mhath! (Lawrence Schimel and Elīna Brasliņa, Scottish Gaelic translation by Marcas Mac an Tuairneir, 2023)

FORTHCOMING

William Soutar: Collected Works, Volume 1, Published Poetry (1923-1946) (Paul S Philippou (Editor-in-Chief) & Kirsteen McCue and Philippa Osmond-Williams (editors), 2023)

William Soutar: Collected Works, Volume 2, Published Poetry (1948-2000) (Paul S Philippou (Editor-in-Chief) & Kirsteen McCue and Philippa Osmond-Williams (editors), 2023)

The Stone of Destiny & The Scots (John Hulbert, 2023)

The Mysterious Case of the Stone of Destiny: A Scottish Historical Detective Whodunnit! (David Maule, 2023)

A History of Irish Republicanism in Dundee, c1840 to 1985 (Rút Nic Foirbais, 2023)

The Whole Damn Town (Hannah Ballantyne, 2024)

Balkan Rhapsody (Maria Kassimova-Moisset, translated by Iliyana Nedkova Byrne, 2024)

The Black Watch from the Crimean War to the Second Boer War (Derek Patrick and Fraser Brown, 2024)

William Soutar: Collected Works, Volume 3 (Miscellaneous & Unpublished Poetry) (Paul S Philippou (Editor-in-Chief) & Kirsteen McCue and Philippa Osmond-Williams (editors), 2024)

William Soutar: Collected Works, Volume 4 (Prose Selections) (Paul S Philippou (Editor-in-Chief) & Kirsteen McCue and Philippa Osmond-Williams (editors), 2025)

All Tippermuir Books titles are available from bookshops and online booksellers. They can also be purchased directly (with free postage & packing (UK only) – minimum charges for overseas delivery) from

www.tippermuirbooks.co.uk.

Tippermuir Books Ltd can be contacted at

mail@tippermuirbooks.co.uk